# Social Media and the Value of Truth

# Social Media and the Value of Truth

## Edited by Berrin Beasley and
## Mitchell R. Haney

LEXINGTON BOOKS
Lanham • Boulder • New York • Toronto • Plymouth, UK

Published by Lexington Books
A wholly owned subsidiary of The Rowman & Littlefield Publishing Group, Inc.
4501 Forbes Boulevard, Suite 200, Lanham, Maryland 20706
www.rowman.com

10 Thornbury Road, Plymouth PL6 7PP, United Kingdom

British Library Cataloguing in Publication Information Available

**Library of Congress Cataloging-in-Publication Data**
Social media and the value of truth / edited by Berrin Beasley and Mitchell R. Haney.
pages cm.
Includes bibliographical references and index.
ISBN 978-0-7391-7412-8 (cloth : alk. paper) -- ISBN 978-0-7391-7413-5 (electronic)
1. Mass media--Moral and ethical aspects. 2. Social media--Moral and ethical aspects. I. Beasley,
Berrin, 1970- II. Haney, Mitchell R., 1967-
P94.S63 2013
302.23--dc23
2012040177

™
The paper used in this publication meets the minimum requirements of American
National Standard for Information Sciences Permanence of Paper for Printed Library
Materials, ANSI/NISO Z39.48-1992.

Printed in the United States of America

# Contents

# Preface

This volume grew out of the Third Annual A. David Kline Symposium on Public Philosophy held in Jacksonville, Florida in the fall of 2010. The annual symposium, supported by the Florida Blue Center for Ethics, brings together leading scholars on an issue of public concern to discuss with their peers their views on said issue with the final aim of dissemination in the form of a volume such as this. The 2010 symposium brought together leading scholars from Communication, Journalism, and Philosophy to discuss issues on the role of social media in contemporary life with reference to its effects on the value of truth. This volume is the culmination of those discussions.

We would like to thank Dr. Alissa Swota, Co-Director of the Florida Blue Center for Ethics, for her continued support of the A. David Kline Symposium on Public Philosophy which laid the grounds for this volume. We want, in addition, to thank Dr. Hans Herbert Koegler, Chair of the Department of Philosophy and Religious Studies, and Dr. David Goff, Chair of Department of Communication, for all their support of this year's symposium. We would also like to thank Jeannemarie Celentano and Robert Holtzman for all their help in logistical support throughout the event. I would like to personally thank Dr. Berrin Beasley for all her efforts both with regards to the symposium and to this volume. Her efforts are truly appreciated.

Mitchell R. Haney, Associate Professor of Philosophy and Co-Director of the Florida Blue Center for Ethics

# Introduction

## Berrin Beasley

A brief history of social media reminds us that it truly is a brief one, because social media have been with us less than twenty years. It was 1994 when TheGlobe.com introduced internet users to a place where they could customize their identity by sharing contact information and photos and interacting with others through chat rooms and instant messaging. Unfortunately, TheGlobe.com shuttered its site in 2008, another victim of MySpace and Facebook, but what it brought to the internet and its staggering number of users was a location for personal expression where others could experience that expression, whether by simply reading the content or participating in its creation.

In the eighteen years since TheGlobe first appeared, a surfeit of social networking sites has come and gone, taking with them bits and pieces of our lives. What have we learned from their arrivals and departures? That most social networking sites have short lives, and in return for participating in them we must shorten our lives accordingly. We are limited to brief status updates, 140-character tweets, and spurts of conversations using emoticons to convey feelings not easily expressed in truncated communication. We've also learned that, for better or worse, social media affect us and our relationships with others and therefore require a deeper contemplation than the social media format itself allows. This book is intended to assist with that deeper contemplation.

The first section of the book addresses the ways in which we define ourselves or are defined by our social media use. Kathy Richardson explores the blurring of Erving Goffman's front-stage/back-stage personas on social media sites, concluding that this blurring raises issues about the ability of users to discern what is appropriate information and behavior for the front stage as opposed to that of the back stage. Deni Elliott writes about the ways in which social media sites literally define us and how our use of anonymity and pseudonymity are altered by the sites themselves.

The second section of the book explores the concept of authentic living. Paul Bloomfield examines individuals' participation in massive multi-player online games like World of Warcraft and Second Life and how one's real life can become subjugated to the life of one's avatar. Mitch Haney also writes on the importance of living an authentic life and concludes that the very speed of social media use, a speed often defined by the site itself, prevents users from reflecting on their lives and making deliberate choices about the objects and projects for which they truly care. Vance Ricks examines some of the possible social and political consequences of gossip spread via social media and how the meaning of gossip may be affected by the very nature of social media.

The final section of the book is applied in purpose. It reflects the practical application of social media in a world saturated by professional media. Lee Wilkins addresses the concept of liquid journalism, where social media users share with traditional journalists the responsibility of gathering and exchanging information and of bringing back emotion to the news. Jane Kirtley ends the book with the reminder that no matter how entertaining or informing social media may be, there are always legal considerations related to its use, especially that of making money.

Social media may have developed from a desire for personal connection, but the result has become a complex account of mediated participation unparalleled by previous communication methods. These intricate individual and corporate media representations and practices call for careful consideration at this stage in the development of social media, which is what this book attempts to do in some small way. We have purposely crossed academic boundaries by bringing together scholarship from the disciplines of communication and philosophy to illustrate the far-reaching implications of this new expression format. By their very nature social media rapidly evolve, training users to quickly move on to the next new site. In some ways they redirect our presentation of self, in others our knowing of self. We hope that by focusing on a few of the issues surrounding social media use we may contribute to a better understanding of its ethical challenges.

*I*

# Constructing an Online Identity

*Chapter One*

# Front-Stage and Back-Stage Kantian Ethics

## Promoting Truth and Trust in Social Media Communities

## Kathy Brittain Richardson

Truthful communication in the complex, changing, connected worlds of social media is as essential—albeit more complicated—as truth telling in traditional communities. Truth and trust have long been intertwined within human communication and communities and have been deemed as an essential for community life, creating the "mutual 'faithfulness' on which all social relationships ultimately depend" (Lewis and Weigert, p. 968). As moralist Sissela Bok (1978) writes, "A society, then, whose members were unable to distinguish truthful messages from deceptive ones, would collapse" (1978, p. 20). The Kantian principle of humanity that demands that truth be the basis for ethical human interactions among rational beings is applicable to social media communications. The practice of individual truth telling can adapt to this user-created environment when those persons practice an ethic of truthful creative consistency in which no *false* personal information is shared without acknowledgement of such invention and when the individual user is allowed to make choices about what truthful personal information is shared within or across the environment. In this way, the characteristics of truthfulness, mutuality, respect and trust that distinguished civil communications and established communities before the web emerged can and must become part of the ethic of life in virtual networks or "villages" as well.

## LIFE IN THE VIRTUAL VILLAGE

To illustrate this point, imagine online communities as a type of virtual village[1] created by and within various types of social media—a village inhabited by those who are active within social networks or blogosphere and those who are voluntarily or involuntarily positioned there, "groups of people with common interests and practices that communicate regularly and for some duration in an organized way over the Internet through a common location or mechanism" (Ridings, Gefen and Arinze, 2002, p. 273). Within the village, the residents gather deliberately or inadvertently, regularly or somewhat haphazardly. Just as in a physical village or city, the inhabitants, their motivations and their gratifications, vary. Some enter the village to work or to play. Some go to promote or to sell. Others enter with loud announcements of their presence; others move quietly or lurk in the shadows. Some are circumspect with their public communications; others aggressively assert political, religious, social or economic positions.

Some communicate as virtual nudists revealing all details and information about themselves and others. Others reveal little, lurking as virtual Peeping Toms, visiting the community only to gaze voyeuristically or commercially through openings at the interactions of other represented selves. A few are there to steal or to attack. Celebrities, politicians, leaders, publicity seekers, business people, artists, commercial interests; organizations and partisans; ghostwriters; children; adults; men and women share the place and the space. Some are aware of their presence within the virtual community; others may be unknowing or unknown.

And, even those who have not willingly joined or entered or networked may find themselves within the village or community. Their photos may be tagged; their activities may be videotaped and uploaded directly to YouTube. Their words, their expressions, their occurrences, their realities no longer belong to them or are controlled by them. Others make the choice to link them, connect them, edit them, broadcast them—and no consent is necessary for any of it to occur. Thus, all are subject to being digitally and socially expressed. All may be joined to this new social space, even though entry was not voluntary.

Life within the virtual village appears to be both highly public and highly privatized. None of what one posts or tweets is secret or exclusive, though users may believe they are sharing only with those who have politely knocked and been admitted through virtual doorways. At best, users share with those within a selective network; yet even then, data are accessible by the hosts, those who built and maintain the infrastructure that supports the virtual dwelling places, and may be used by them to target individuals for specific marketing appeals. It is a community of exchange and contribution, but it can also be a site for surreptitious surveillance, data theft or unauthorized sharing because, for the most part, security is based solely on the good will of those within the village. There are no authorized police, few effective locks and infrequent or ineffective punishments.

At its most public, the communication is open to whoever chooses to look. Users learn who is eating lunch where, whose children are playing soccer where, what employee is about to be fired, and who is bored at work. Villagers may know when people are online and when they are not, where they are checking in and who is with them there, and with instantaneous, streaming status updates, the nuances of every event, every emotion and, perhaps, every thought that occurs within the digital social world can be shared and archived for what seems to be eternal access. When traditional gatekeeping gives way to virtual "over-the-fence" gossip that may travel hundreds of miles in a second along a digital chain, and graffiti that once may have been spray painted on an old railcar is instead posted on a Facebook wall, truthfulness and trustworthiness in content and context take on larger—wider—and perhaps more lasting consequence.

## KANTIAN ETHICS IN THE SOCIAL MEDIA CONTEXT

One might conjecture that philosopher Immanuel Kant would find such open, transparent sharing of truth idyllic. The deontological philosopher under-stood truth to be the bond tying together all rational human society. Truthful communication, he believed, was innately good and instrumentally good—the necessary component of all human interaction (1797/1991, p. 52). Telling the truth was an inescapable duty of each human being because offering truth to others affirms their innate worthiness and dignity as rational beings and enables them to make free and reasoned choices. Such a duty to others is not lessened by the communication or social context, according to Kant, because truthful communication inherently creates conditions in which social order and community can flourish. To deny anyone truth in public communication "violates the human duty toward others" (p. 427) and to oneself, he argued. Treating others as less than worthy of the truth reduces them to objects, a violation of the categorical imperative intended to guide virtuous behavior; persons should never be treated as means to an end, regardless of the per-ceived worth of the end (1785/2002). Thus, the constant stream of informa-tion offered through social media to anyone who cares to attend to it and the many ways in which online communities can act quickly to correct falsity would find great justification within Kant's deontological principles of duty-bound truth telling.

However, such crowd-sourced validity checking does not identify, coun-ter or stop the deliberate dissemination of false or invasive information, and therefore the issue of online falsity and harm in social media must be addressed. Kant's system of deontological ethics offers no ethical justification for those who knowingly post or share false or satirical information—even if it were in an attempt to be entertaining or funny—if it would be likely that users or readers would *believe* it to be truthful and therein be deceived. In his value system, the only justifiable lie is one uttered as an unmistakable joke or boast—and then only when it is clearly understood by all to be a jest, rather than an assertion of fact. From this perspective, the context of an online disclosure becomes as critical as the content. For example, someone who creates a fictional self-representation while engaging in an online game or virtual reality setting in which all players knowingly assume new identities as avatars with fictional gender, names, personal traits or experiences is not practicing deception. However, a researcher assuming a false identity as someone recently diagnosed with a disease in order to gather qualitative data about reactions to diagnoses and illnesses on a medical message board intended for patients and their families would be engaged in a non-justifiable deception.

## THE NATURE OF TRUTH AND TRUST IN SOCIAL MEDIA COMMUNITIES

But does one have to tell "nothing but the truth" to function virtuously in the virtual village? Would it be deceptive to reveal only part of the truth about oneself on a social network or other digital setting, under a Kantian ethic, or to choose a representation (profile icon or photo) that lacks true authenticity? The categorical imperative of Kant calls on one to act—in this case, to communicate—in the manner in which he or she believes that everyone should in a similar situation. From this perspective, it would be morally justifiable to share information selectively—perhaps even advisable to protect privacy or safety in some settings—as long as what is shared is truthful and not intended to mistreat, objectify or create injustice for others in the setting. If the persona created online and shared publicly is not misleading in that it is all truthful but not all complete, then such might be deemed universally acceptable. But this is at best creative disclosure as one chooses the truths about oneself that will be shared without divulging *too* much, and so moral caution must remain. In such cases, a commitment to consistency in such representation—telling the same truth consistently without mixing it with wishful aspirations, deliberate deception or willful harm—seems demanded by Kantian ideals. And, even then, the amount of truth disclosed or withheld should be carefully weighed to maximize transparency within the context. The practice of truthful creative consistency can only be justified if it is used when and in situations that could be deemed ethical for everyone in that virtual space, and not when it is solely for ease or to craft online personas that mislead, harm or use others for one's own gain or amusement. For all users to interact effectively in the virtual social world and to contribute to its ongoing maintenance, they must at some level be able to accept what is represented there as truthful and to accord information, opinions and emotions shared as some form of authentic expression. In fact, the very nature of the virtual social encounter should prompt an even higher commitment to truth telling than traditional social encounters since it would be easier for firsthand experience to uncover falsehoods or reveal deception.

Therefore, one must consider the needs of the individual and the social organization as one decides how much truthfulness is required for humans to flourish in digital communities through digital communications. Truth telling is at its most essential when the shared information is used for critical decision making, as in cases involving political, economic, medical and familial matters, but it is still important when it might affect the trustworthiness of the communication exchange. Even a small lie is a lie; many small lies may disrupt or destroy even the most stable relationship, as most certainly the great lie will. Similarly, the courage to tell some truths is found only when those who receive it are willing to safeguard and protect it.

Perhaps some of the difficulty or challenge in practicing both truth telling and trustworthiness in social media comes from the undefined nature of the social space: Is it public or private? Or, in extending the village metaphor, do open doors signal that one should feel free to come in and take whatever is available for one's use? Do residents fail to hang curtains over their windows because they feel very secure—or because they want to be seen in all situations? Sociologist Erving Goffman (1959, 1963) drew from the language of the theatre to describe how awareness of the public and social nature of a space seemed to determine the boundaries for individual actions within that space. Just as actors in a stage production understand the differences in "front stage" performances when an audience is present and "back stage" preparation and relaxation behaviors, Goffman argued that the front, public region for social exchange is bounded by standards of politeness and decorum developed through a personal understanding of one's moral obligations and the instrumental requirements of the social group. But backstage, individuals step away from the public persona they have created and feel free to ad lib, relax and change characters, costumes and makeup. Meyrowitz (1985) drew from Goffman's work to describe the profound change in understanding of psychological and social spaces—front stage and back stage—he believed to be prompted by the electronic immersion of American culture. Electronic media had "moved the dividing line between private and public behavior" (p. 308), allowing the viewing child to enter suddenly into the adult world and viewing adults to enter into social spaces once thought to be unvaryingly private. As more and more of the physical and social world becomes an electronically created public stage, the potential for safeguarding a relaxed or preparatory back stage area related to social role fades, leaving at least some viewers with *No Sense of Place*, the evocative title of Meyrowitz's 1985 book. However, even though the video world tore the curtain away from the front and backstage representations of those captured by the camera lens, viewers were not themselves so caught. While watching others' public and private lives might cause one to lose respect for government officials or become entranced with actors, the personal boundaries did not shift without consent or knowledge. Even those caught on "Candid Camera" had to grant permission for their situations to be aired, and performers on reality television and talk shows still offer some form of consent for their experiences to become public.

In contrast, social media by their very nature blur distinctions between private and public behavior, raising issues about the understanding of appropriate disclosures within the communication and social environment and questions about what is truthful and responsible. *All* social media communication in some sense requires public representations, yet the communications are formed and shared within what may be a confusing mix of public and private space with no apparent curtain or controllable stage. Too often, spontaneous, unplanned and out-of-character communication and actions better suited for backstage display only become highly public on the front stage of the web, perhaps deliberately, perhaps accidentally. The speed, permeability and viral nature of the web and the digital cloud allow for very few curtains between front stage and backstage activities or presentations, and the social actors often have no direction, cues or scripts to follow to provide guidance for their performances.

One great difference from previous media that social media present is the openness of the function of director. Technology allows anyone who wants to do so to create and edit videos, photos or illustrations and to post or share them in multiple settings. The electronic media analyzed by Meyrowitz and the interpersonal or small-group encounters studied by Goffman did not allow anyone to take charge of the communication in similar ways, and this capability poses even more challenge to one's sense of place or sense of decorum. While deliberate users know when they are "on Facebook" or "on Twitter" as they create personal accounts, post individual profiles, accept friends or followers, and agree to privacy and use guidelines, they are making deliberate choices about representations. However, others may be unaware of being photographed or videotaped and uploaded. Actions or communications they believe to be occurring backstage may instead become a global performance. The "audience" for the performances or messages may have little to no opportunities to engage in actual interactions that allow for verification of anything that is posted, shared or stored, and they may not be told about the lack of knowledge or consent of those engaged in the suddenly front-stage communication. In the best case, as one is online with others, chatting or interacting, one might encounter an almost instantaneous corrective to false or inappropriate postings from the "audience." In other scenarios, however, one might be encouraged to go even further into deception, cheered on by the laughter and approval of onlookers interested in flashy or shocking entertainment and forgetting about potential impact on others.

Such may have been true for the Rutgers roommate convicted in 2012 of using a webcam to stream live visuals of a date his gay roommate had in their room for those he had invited on Twitter to watch. It is highly likely he did not consider the impact sharing the webcast with other students would have on his roommate, who committed suicide a few days later by jumping off the George Washington Bridge (Zernike, 16 March 2012). Was the content of the webcast truthful? Perhaps. But capturing even truthful information in a context of deception and using the web to make the private quite public cannot be justified—and in this case led to a criminal conviction for one and perhaps prompted the death of another.

Consider another incident in which backstage behavior and information became highly public without consent: In 2010, Karen Owens, a Duke female graduate, created a "fake thesis" complete with slides and charts detailing sexual encounters with 13 identified Duke athletes and circulated it through email to a few friends. Unfortunately the friends in turn circulated it, and within days and without Owens' consent—or that of the athletes—the photos and graphs went viral. They were posted by a recipient on the Deadspin and Jezebel websites and circulated on Twitter (Seelye and Robbins, 2010). What was intended as a humorous message for a small audience of friends then was shared with thousands of viewers, opening not only the life of the young woman to public scrutiny and criticism but also those of the 13 young men she included in her account, their teams, and the university itself. Again, the information contained in the "fake thesis" may be wholly or partially true, but the truthful content does not justify disseminating it without consent in a front-stage context for which it was never intended.

The volume of information shared through social media may itself distort or decontextualize truth from its original public or private area. What is posted or uploaded seems to be ever present, mixing what may be no longer accurate with what may be accurate for the specific moment to such a degree that all is misunderstood. Irate postings after an argument, emotional reactions to public events, even photographs or videos once accurate may lose their truthfulness as circumstances and contexts change. Unfortunately, the same technologies that enable virtually instantaneous communications may also mean that no communication is ever truly erased. Thus, time and age may have little relevance to the public communications shared within the virtual village. Corporate recruiters have grown used to a Google or Bing search or to searching Facebook or other virtual networks to find information about applicants, and information or photos posted long ago—or those posted by someone else—can affect hiring decisions (Finder, 2005 June 11). Mashable.com (Warren, 2011 June 16) described "10 People Who Have Lost Their Jobs Over Social Media Mistakes," including a high school teacher fired after posting a Facebook photo of herself with an alcoholic drink, even though there were privacy restrictions on accessing the page. The choices of virtual representation and misrepresentation—and the clash of front-stage and back-stage behaviors made possible by the web—loom large in a digital world in which analog temporality has vanished and data seem to be eternally present and available.

Overtly false front-stage representation in social media may be too easy. Consider these examples of Twitter use in which actual identities are exchanged for the virtual:

- A Twitter feed @JBK1960 is supposedly coming from Jackie Kennedy Onassis (Young, 2010 Sept. 20). In all actuality, the John F. Kennedy Presidential Library started the Twitter account using information drawn from a weekly column written by Mrs. Kennedy during her husband's presidential campaign.
- Celebrities and politicians, from President Obama and Ron Paul (Rich, 2010 Oct. 9, paras. 4-5), to Britney Spears and rapper 50 Cent (Cohen, 2009 March 27) reportedly regularly use ghost writers to develop Tweets for their Twitter accounts.
- A falsely identified Twitter account, @BPGlobalPR, satirized the giant petroleum corporation as it dealt with the aftermath of a tragic oil spill in the Gulf of Mexico; the satirical account apparently gained four times more followers than did the real corporate account (Heussner, 2010 May 25).

Unfortunately, the ease of anonymity for users and viewers may allow performers and audiences to forget that others may assume new identities in the public spaces of social networks and message boards, deceiving other users by adopting names, characteristics or experiences that are inherently false. Consider the impact of such deception in the case of Megan Meier, a 13-year-old who committed suicide after being bullied on her MySpace page by a neighborhood mother who, along with her 13-year-old daughter and another adult friend, had been posing as a young man to trick Meier (Maag, 2007 Dec. 11). Meier had been unhappy at school, but had thought she would find friends online. Instead, she was duped into believing a young man was interested in her, only to then be dropped by him with a note that said, "The world would be a better place without you." The messages came not from a young man, however, but from the online poser. Meier responded to the electronic breakup with a note that said, "You're the kind of boy a girl would kill herself over." Her suicide followed (Steinhauer, 2008 Nov. 27, paras. 10-

11). This incident provides a tragic illustration of the ease with which one may assume false identities online and the Kantian warning against the untrue jest that is not understood by all.

It is well worth noting that the concerns raised by Meyrowitz about the loss of childhood innocence prompted by televised access to unfiltered backstage adult behaviors are exacerbated by the open nature of web communication. Social media have made it very easy for minors to access virtually all outlets in the same way as adults. The anonymity of digital communication may prevent others from recognizing the age or vulnerability of those engaging in the virtual exchanges. But, when such is known, it is important to be truthful, non-deceptive and mindful of the duty owed those who may be far more trusting than adults in similar settings. The communities of social media may be virtual, but the emotional impact of the communication may be all too real. It is, after all, the communication that *is* the real component of the virtual village, and therefore it is critical that the ethical principles of truth telling and trustworthiness that underlie civil social discourse and social organization in the "real world" should apply to virtual discourse there as well.

Such a core commitment to truth telling provides a necessary component for acts that provide mutual benefit within the community, according to the call for communitarian practices in ethical communication expressed by Christians, Ferré and Fackler (1993; Christians, Fackler and Ferré, 2012). The type of communication that best promotes this mutuality, Christians, Ferré and Fackler assert, is a "rich concept of truthful narrative" (1993, p. 119), accounts that accurately and deeply contextualize, probe, and make meaning of events and processes. Obviously, virtual networks offer an accessible, affordable and easy venue for such truthful narratives, with unprecedented opportunity for multiple voices to introduce and challenge multiple perspectives in ways beyond the reach of traditional news media or even town-hall meetings or forums. From Twitter and Tumblr streams as breaking news events occur to comments posted throughout the day on a Facebook wall, the virtual village provides the opportunity for crowdsourced and crowd verified social accounts that occur in real time. Personal histories and narratives take on more richness and depth as they are shared through multimedia, with commentary and reaction from others. Political opinions shared through blogs may be challenged, supported or extended beyond the one viewpoint to reflect the many, offering a more complete "marketplace of ideas" for those interested in seeking or promoting truth.

Such truthful narratives shared through social media can offer truth and build trust. During the late summer 2010 Four Mile Canyon wildfire near Boulder, Colorado, social media were used to promote and provide this type of truthful "rich narrative" that served to unite and protect a real community. David Wild's blog, *allhazards.blogspot.com*, identified numerous sources of real-time information about where the fire was moving, evacuations, police and firefighter activity, shelter and support efforts. Twitter streams at #boulderfire kept residents informed of the direction and severity of the fires. Maps, photos and analysis were available through Flickr, YouTube, various personal and organizational web pages and blogs that were updated continuously. The event, the aftermath and the recovery were crowdsourced by residents, safety professionals, weather authorities and others, allowing the community to work together to keep its residents as safe and informed as possible.

In such settings, the social order is maintained, not by external bodies or rules, but by the communications of the participants as they interact, opine, negotiate, challenge, trade, disagree and support each other. For example, the call for users themselves to create a Council on Ethical Blogging and Aggregation that will establish standards for aggregation of other people's content online, announced by Simon Dumenco at the 2012 South by Southwest Interactive festival (Carr, 2012 March 11), illustrates how new cultural orders can be developed that will offer guidance for appropriate and truthful representations online. Similarly, agreement on protocols for disclosure and consent in online representations, signs for use when participants in virtual games or discussion groups or sites do not anticipate or want truthful disclosures (the Kantian "jest"), and ways to report or to act against abuses of the front-stage/back-stage dynamic can be reached by rational beings who are truthful with each other and who choose to act in ways they would want each social network member to follow.

Imagine again life in the virtual village if residents and visitors were to accept their duty to engage in truthful disclosure or creative consistencies. Deceptive communications from individuals or organizations that promote self-centeredness at the expense of the communal good would be limited or banned; explicit personal communications that disturb the peace or disrupt civil discourse would similarly be curbed. Posting embarrassing or harmful material about others within the village without their consent would be seen as an affront, even if it is thought to be truthful, because it uses others as objects of ridicule. When an individual posts personal information about himself or herself that may be harmful, others in the community would act on their behalf, warning them of potential hazards—because they would want someone to do the same for them. In such a way, those who engage in the village dialogue could function as the virtual "Neighborhood Watch," seeking to preserve the safety and peace of the village through cooperation and mutuality. The creation of new online identities through masked identities may be tolerated only if and when the identities are not used to harm others or the community itself. Communicators could share information based on consideration of the needs of self and others, affirmatively sharing hard truths when they would contribute to mutuality and choosing not to share information that is at best purely trivial and at worst prurient. Thus, life in the village would again be bounded and shaped by understandings of mutual needs and civic etiquette in ways that promote truthfulness and trust within the virtual village, and the uneasy obligations of the simultaneous virtual user/performer and audience member could be tempered by the creation of restraint—a curtain of sorts—that acknowledges and even celebrates a separation of the front-stage and back-stage performance, the intentional public from the private. In this environment, the principles of Kant applied within a communitarian commitment would promote truthfulness and trustworthiness among residents and visitors to the digital village.

## NOTE

1. The village metaphor is drawn from the early writing of Marshall McLuhan, who described such a new space in which the divisions that had separated cultures and geographies would fall as "the electro-magnetic discoveries have recreated the simultaneous 'field' in all human affairs so that the human family now exists under conditions of a 'global village'" (1962, p. 31).

## REFERENCES

Bok, S. (1978). *Lying. Moral choice in public and private life.* New York: Vintage Books.

Carr, D. (2012 March 11). A code of conduct for content aggregators. *The New York Times.* http://www.nytimes.com/2012/03/12/business/media/guideliens-proposed-for-content-aggregation-online.html?

Christians, C.G., Fackler, P.M., & Ferré, J.P. (2012). *Ethics for public communication.* New York: Oxford Univ. Press.

Christians, C.G., Ferré, J.P., & Fackler, P.M. (1993). *Good news: Social ethics and the press.* New York: Oxford Univ. Press.

Cohen, N. (2009 March 27). When stars twitter, a ghost may be lurking. *The New York Times,* A-1.

Finder, A. (2005 June 11). When a risque online persona undermines a chance for a job. *The New York Times,* Section 1, p. 1.

Goffman, E. (1963). *Behavior in public places.* Westport, CT: Greenwood Press.

Goffman, E. (1959, 1973). *The presentation of self in everyday life.* Woodstock, NY: The Overlook Press.

Heussner, K.M. (2010 May 25). Fake BP Twitter account mocks oil spill PR efforts. ABC News. http://abcnews.go.com/Technology.fake-bp-twitter-account-mocks-oil-spill-opr?story?id=1...

Kant, I. (1785/2002). *Groundwork for the metaphysics of morals.* A.W. Wood, (Ed. Trans.). Cambridge: Cambridge University Press.

Kant, I. (1797/1991). *The metaphysics of morals.* (M. Gregor, Trans.). Cambridge: Cambridge University Press.

Kant, I. (1997). *Lectures on ethics.* Peter Heath and J.B. Schneewind (Eds). (P. Heath, Trans.). Cambridge, England: Cambridge Univ. Press.

Lewis, J.D. & Weigert, A. (1985 June). Trust as a social reality. *Social Forces, 63*(4), 967-985.

Maag, C. (2007 Dec. 16). When the bullies turned faceless. *The New York Times,* Style, p. 9. Retrieved from Lexisnexis.com.

McLuhan, M. (1962). *The Gutenberg galaxy.* Toronto: Univ. of Toronto Press.

Meyrowitz, J. (1985) *No sense of place: The impact of electronic media on social behavior.* New York: Oxford Univ. Press.

Rich, F. (2010 October 9). Facebook politicians are not your friends. *The New York Times.* http:www.nytimes.com/2010/10/10/opinion/10rich.html?th=&emc=th&pagewanted=print

Ridings, C.M., Gefen, D., & Arinze, B. (2002). Some antecedents and effects of trust in virtual communities. *Journal of Strategic Information Systems, 11*, 271-295.

Rosen, J. (19 July 2010). The web means the end of forgetting. *The New York Times Magazine.* http://www.nytimes.com/2010/07/25/magazine/25privacy-t2.html?pagewanted=all

Seelye, K.Q., & Robbins, L. (2010 October 7). Duke winces as a private joke slips out of control. *The New York Times.* http://www.nytimes.com/2010/10/08/us/08duke.htmlsq=duke sexscandal&st=cse&scp=...

Steinhauer, J. (2008 Nov. 27). Verdict in MySpace suicide case. *The New York Times.* http://www.nytimes.com/2008/11/27/us/27myspace.html?_r=1&pagewanted=print .

Warren, C. (2011 June 16). 10 people who have lost jobs over social media mistakes. Mashable.com. http://mashable.com/2011/06/16/weignergate-social-media-job-loss/ .

Young, S. (2010 Sept. 20). Jackie Kennedy's on Twitter—creepy or cool? Associated Press.

Zernike, K. (16 March 2012). Defendant in Rutgers spying case guilty of hate crimes. *The New York Times,* Section 1, P. 1.

*Chapter Two*

# The Real Name Requirement and Ethics of Online Identity

## Deni Elliott

The online Nym War had been waging for a decade before what came to be known as the Final Identity Battle (FIB) in the summer of 2011. The battle-field was the newly created Google+ social network site. As virtually bloody as any 666 online game, this battle threatened to shatter the boundary between the virtual and the physical world. The Nym War left real people bandaging their hurt, frustration and confusion, even as they remained steadfast in their united determination to continue to pseudonymously live an active online life while keeping their physical life identities hidden from the virtual world of advertisers, administrators and users. Both sides in this controversy, the website administrators on one side and those taking part in the pseudonymous revolt on the other, knew that this battle was different from those in the past. Before, it had been possible to simply boycott sites that insisted on "real name" disclosure. But, Google controlled too much virtual real estate for those who made their living online or spent substantial a-vocational time online for these users to collect their profile and go elsewhere, no matter how easy Google made the "take out" procedure.

In this chapter, I use Google+'s real name requirement to demonstrate ethical analysis of online controversy. I distinguish among the concepts of anonymity, pseudonymity, and confidentiality in online communication and argue that the burden of justification is on those who would demand disclosure of identity rather than those who seek to protect it. I take a look at who is harmed and who benefits from online real name requirements. I conclude by showing that twenty-first century web-based mass communication ethics requires systematic analysis based on common morality in contrast with the twentieth century model of professionally-based media ethics.

## THE REAL NAME REQUIREMENT AND GOOGLE+

Google's new social network, Google+, launched in June 2011. Its description, "real life sharing rethought for the web," gives a banal feel to the newest in the Google lineup of more than 150 desktop, mobile, and online products. But, embedded in the new platform was a massive change that resulted in individuals providing an unprecedented amount of information about themselves to what has become the world's largest and most diverse corporation. In the past, Google had allowed individuals to use any name that they wanted in creating profiles on many of its products, such as Gmail and YouTube. But, when individuals signed up for the new social network platform, they were required to provide their "common names." Once one has created a Google+ profile with one's "common name" the corporation then substitutes the Google+ profile for any previous profiles in the Google system.

Google's search engine, the most used worldwide, has been collecting and aggregating information since 1999 and continues to build its knowledge through 1 billion searches each day (Wikipedia, 2012). As of March 2012, Google had acquired, "on average, more than one company per month since 2010" (Wikipedia, 2012) with the acquisitions—now numbering more than 100—spanning all elements of computer technology and services, along with diversification into biotechnology firms and utilities. As the content and patterns of Gmail, web searches, YouTube use, Googledocs, and RSS feeds have been collected and aggregated by the corporation beginning in 1999, the introduction of the Google+ social network provided the company the new opportunity to attach all of that data to the user's physical world identity.

Google explained the new requirement this way: "Google+ makes connecting with people on the web more like connecting with people in the real world. Because of this, it's important to use your common name so that people you want to connect with can find you. Your common name is the name your friends, family or co-workers usually call you" (Google, 2011).

If Google+ became a successful competitor to Facebook, it had the potential of shaping the future of online interaction. Bloggers, entrepreneurial journalists, and others dependent on their developed online presence could predict that not being part of the new social network was likely to interfere with their ability to connect with their audiences and advertisers.

According to an early review of Google+ by Techcrunch blogger MG Seigler, "Google+ is more than a social product, or even a social strategy, it's an extension of Google itself...It's through Circles that users select and organize contacts into groups for optimal sharing....With Sparks, you enter an interest you have and Google goes out and finds elements on the web that they think you'll care about. These can be links to blog posts, videos, books – anything that Google searches for." As Seigler breathlessly tells us, "The key to the [Google+] project is the attempt to unify everything" (Seigler, 2011).

Despite Seigler's enthusiasm for the new social network, the blogger would soon find that s/he would not be able to sign up for Google+ using the name under which s/he blogs, MG Seigler. According to the Google+ rules, "Names that consist primarily of initials . . . are not allowed in the first or last name fields" (Google, 2011).

## LOGICAL PROBLEM OF THE REAL NAME REQUIREMENT

A process is overly exclusive if it inappropriately excludes those outside of the set intended to be left out. The Google+ real name requirement is overly exclusive in that it does not allow people to enroll with their real names if that names do not fit the dominant society views of what Google's software engineers think counts as a name. A Google+ profile name includes a call name and a surname. The requirement excludes those from cultures, such as Mongolia, who normally do not have two separate names, along with others who have been given or have chosen a single "legal" name, or that include initials as a first or last name, or that include "special" symbols (Google, 2011). So, ultimately, what Google+ demands is a name that sounds common enough for the software engineers. Ironically, that means that some people can enroll only if they create fake names that fit Google+ standards.

The real name requirement is also not clear about just what counts as one's real (or common name). Google+ would argue that a person's common name is synonymous with one's legal name—the name that appears on a birth certificate, social security card, the name that an individual is known by. Unfortunately, for some people, these might be three different names. In some cultures, for example, many women have a maiden (birth certificate) name that is different from what appears on their (post-marriage) social security card, which may be entirely different from the (nick)name by which they are known in the physical world.

Last of all, one's common name may be too common to provide unique identification online. My friend, Sue Smith, is indistinguishable from thousands of others with the same name. But, if Sue's online persona profile listed her as Gulfcoasthorseenthusiast, it would distinguish her, in at least a couple of ways, from many of the other Sue Smiths.

## ANONYMITY, PSEUDONYMITY, CONFIDENTIALITY

Anonymity derives from the Greek "no name" while pseudonymity derives from the Greek "false name." Anonymity is usually attached to an event or singular situation. The whistleblower anonymously mails documents to the

*New York Times* with no return address. A restaurant owner anonymously posts a scathing review of a competitor, which is an ethically questionable act known as "astroturfing."

Pseudonymity presents a persona, which is usually persistent over time and events, in which the alternate identity is held separate from one's common or legal identity. One may build credibility, relationships, and a large set of fans with a pseudonym, as we know from Mark Twain, Dr. Seuss, and a host of celebrities past and present.

Confidentiality is the act of protecting the known identity of another. If I do a blind review of an academic manuscript, the identity of the author is kept confidential by the journal editor and my identity as reviewer is kept confidential as well. Neither of us are anonymous, although we remain unknown to one another, although we share research and analysis with one another.

Anonymity, pseudonymity and confidentiality are morally neutral, in that none of these concepts connotes wrongdoing in a prima facie sense. Anonymity is a voluntary act in which one withholds the identified self from one's act. Pseudonymity is a voluntary act that provides an alternate name or identity to a part of one's self. Confidentiality requires two people in that one guards some piece of another individual's identity or information from others.

Withholding of the identified self may take any of these forms in the virtual world, just as it can in the physical world. One may seek anonymity, pseudonymity or confidentiality for reasons that are morally prohibited, neutral, or permitted. The ethical importance of acts, whether committed by the identified self, anonymous self, pseudonymous self or the self kept confidential by another is whether the intent or content of the act causes unjustified harm to another.

One may be anonymous and pseudonymous to different recipients simultaneously. For example, a hacker will be anonymous to the manager of the secure system she has just breached, but may celebrate her success among her hacker friends who know her pseudonymously. She trusts her life partner to keep her physical world identity confidential from both sets of online users.

Online psychologist John Grohol distinguishes between anonymity and pseudonymity: "Pseudononymous systems strike a balance between people's needs to obscure their identities online, while still allowing them to build reputations in those usernames. These systems have been shown to work very well for an online community" (Grohol, 2006).

Many sites practice confidentiality to protect their users. Users trust information that makes them vulnerable to loss, such as their credit card numbers, to vendor websites with the expectation that the information will not be revealed to others, regardless of the personal or business concern of the other.

It is interesting to note that while complicated "opt out" procedures are the norm for individuals who wish to protect their contact information and consumption habits from being shared by one website with another, the confidentiality of credit card information is assumed by all involved. It would, of course, be ludicrous for online sellers to expect consumers to go through complicated or difficult processes to protect their credit card information. The result would be consumers highly reluctant to make online purchases. The fact that sellers do expect consumers to go through complicated or difficult processes to protect their contact information and consumption habits and that users generally don't bother to protect such information provides evidence for the conclusion that consumers do not yet understand the value of this information in the marketplace.

In the physical world, one does not need to justify withholding one's real name. It is assumed that one has the right to control release of important information about oneself, including one's real name. The burden of justification is on those who would demand to know it. In some situations, it is legally required that one disclose one's real name to verify one's identification, or verification of identification may be required to protect the user in commercial transactions. However, for the most part, we remain anonymous to one another as we pass on city streets. There is no legal or ethical barrier to the adoption of a pseudononymous identity when waiting for one's turn at a restaurant or when joining an affinity group. Conventionally, we expect service providers, such as hair stylists and drycleaners to refrain from gathering and sharing information about us. Legally, such confidentiality is the norm for information gathered by medical and educational personnel.

In the physical world, the burden of justification is not on the individual seeking anonymity, pseudonymity or confidentiality, but rather on those who would deny it. When customers pay cash to buy products in a store, there is no duty for them to disclose their names, phone numbers, or even their zip codes, despite the clerk's request that they do.

The real name requirement is thus ethically questionable first because it incorrectly places the burden of justification on the individual who does not wish to disclose rather than on the organization wishing for disclosure.

# WHO IS HARMED AND WHO BENEFITS FROM THE REAL NAME REQUIREMENTS

## The Argument that Real Names Keep the Internet Safe

Web managers function with the belief that requiring that users reveal their real names cuts down on flaming, trolls, and other uncivil communicative acts. According to online psychologist John Grohol, "Anonymity is a double-edged sword when it comes to an online community. While anonymity may allow people to feel more free and disinhibited to discuss otherwise embarrassing or stigmatizing topics, it can also be a community's biggest enemy. Anonymity allows people to hide behind their computers while saying whatever they want with little ramification. Psychologists know that online community is far more disinhibited than face-to-face communications. Pair that disinhibition with anonymity and you have a recipe for potential disaster" (Grohol, 2006).

Most arguments in favor of real name requirements suggest that people will refrain from engaging in evil acts if their identity is knowable. That claim leads easily to the work of ancient Greek philosopher, Plato, thus illustrating how classic some new media ethical issues turn out to be. In Book II of Plato's Utopian work, *The Republic,* we find Glaucon presenting Socrates with the Myth of Gyges. Gyges, as the story goes, takes a golden ring from a corpse and then finds that when he puts the ring on his finger and turns the ring, he becomes invisible. As the story goes, Gyges uses his new found power to sneak into the Queen's chambers and seduce her; he kills the King and takes over the kingdom. Glaucon uses this story to argue the point that any person would act unjustly if given the chance to do so without consequences. Socrates doesn't directly respond to Glaucon's position until *Book X,* where Socrates formally lays out the argument that people act justly or unjustly because of their character and conscience, not because they will be punished for unjust actions. Most people are familiar with more recent renditions of the Myth of Gyges as it appears in *The Lord of the Rings* and in the *Harry Potter* series.

Socrates' position, that one acts justly just because it is the right thing to do, is also the hallmark of moral sophistication according to contemporary moral developmental theorists. People who are morally mature do the right thing just because it is the right thing to do, not because someone else is watching. The Internet may be the playground of moral ingrates and, depending on which site you peruse, it can certainly seem that way. But, the Internet also provides unprecedented opportunity to teach and learn civility and civic discourse and to appreciate individual and cultural diversity. Rather than creating online environments that operate in the moral basement by requiring real names so that inappropriate users can be more easily caught and punished, online environments should appeal to the best of human nature, by encouraging right acts for the right reasons. The punishment meted out by website administrators is suspension of user privileges and users are suspended regardless of whether they use a real name or not. As users are trusted to provide their real names, it can be assumed that users inclined to act inappropriately may also be willing to lie about their identities. Harms are caused to users by a real name requirement in that it does not appeal to or enhance users' moral development.

## Chilling Effect

Some users claim that a real name requirement causes them harm by restricting them from pursuing interests that they feel unsafe having linked to their physical world identity. Concerns include work-related consequences, or the anticipation of other physical, social, reputational, financial or psychological harm if one's expressed political thoughts, sexual orientation or other online exploration is attached to physical world identity.

Just as the question of what individuals would do if they were not accountable to others led quickly to Plato, the question of harms caused by silencing minority voices leads quickly to nineteenth century British philosopher John Stuart Mill. Mill argued that citizens have the duty to reason carefully about matters of governance and to continually test the validity of one's beliefs against opposing views. He claimed that citizens have a duty "to form the truest opinions they can" (Mill, 1869/1991, p. 59). Citizens achieve that lofty goal by being part of public discussion that includes the hearing of all manner of diverse views, both civil and offensive. Mill notes that most people "have never thrown themselves into the mental position of those who think differently from them and consider what such persons may have to say; consequently, they do not, in any proper sense of the word, know the doctrine which they themselves profess" (pp. 42-43). Having true opinions is essential to the individual becoming educated and enlightened. "The term duty to oneself," Mill said, "when it means anything more than prudence, means self-respect or self-development" (1869, p. 87).

From a Millian perspective, the unjustified harm that an unknowable individual might cause is less than the harm to the community as a whole if diverse voices are silenced or if self-exploration is restricted.

## Governmental Control and Promotion of Democracy

Another problem with the real name requirement is verification. Governmental "real name" requirements that link online user behavior to an individual's governmental ID are abhorrent in most of the world and have been found by the U.S. Supreme Court to be unconstitutional. As of this writing, only China enforces a direct connection between an individual's online action and his or her governmental ID. Without official verification, the real names requirement is more of a real-sounding name request or suggestion. With official verification, citizens run a high risk of having their speech controlled or monitored by those in power. Mill argued that it is not appropriate for government to control objectionable speech, as the temptation for those in power to control dissent was far too great. Mill argued that individuals are not accountable to anyone aside from themselves for how well they do on their personal adventure of self-development (1859, p. 87).

Thus, public discussion and individuals' ability to form true opinion rests on the diversity of views that come when people can speak freely and be exposed to a variety of views different from their own. If a real name requirement interferes with any individual's ability to speak freely, it interferes with the self-development of all and, ultimately, interferes with the democratic process that leads to the aggregate good of the community.

In Mill's companion essay, *Utilitarianism,* he argues that the individual's ability to develop oneself through exposure to different ideas contributes to the good of the community as a whole (1869/1991, p. 142). In an allusion to *On Liberty*, he wrote, "[T]he happiness which forms the utilitarian standard of what is right in conduct, is not the agent's own happiness, but that of all concerned." (1869, p. 148).

Happiness, therefore, is not the product of a passive life in which all of one's desires are met. Rather, happiness is found in the realization of society's shortcomings and active involvement in making the world a better place. There is no better arena for that involvement than the Internet.

A believer in the good of democratic rule, Mill said: "Society between equals can only exist on the understanding that the interests of all are to be regarded equally" (1863, p. 165). But, it is also important not to lose, in the analysis, the reference to the happiness of *all* concerned. Mill's goal is not to have a simple majority of voters calling the shots. Rather, Mill advanced the more sophisticated notion that enlightened self-interest will naturally result in individuals acting for the good of the whole. Regulation of the Internet ought promote democratic interests.

## WHO BENEFITS FROM REAL NAME REQUIREMENTS

If those with unpopular views, and the community that would hear them, are those most harmed by a real name requirement, it is important to consider who might most benefit. The most obvious beneficiaries of an online real name requirement are those with business interests. Google's aggregation data attached to one's physical identity provide a wealth of material that is used to benefit Google and other corporate interests that pay for the privilege of exploiting those data. While Google does have opt-out policies, the complexity of the process guarantees that all but the most motivated user will simply allow Google to do as it wishes with the information. The economic harm caused Google and other corporate interests by denying a real name requirement for the web does not trump the ethical harm caused individuals and the community as a whole by having a real name requirement.

## THE INTERNET, DEMOCRACY, AND CORPORATE INTERESTS

It is true that everyone with access to the Internet can claim a bit of virtual real estate and set up shop, disseminating information and opinion. We can call ourselves journalists or commentators or reviews or bloggers or claim no label at all.

It is also true that the best metaphor for the Internet in its current form is not a "virtual town square," but "virtual Times Square" with a cacophony of advertising on electronic billboards, each demanding attention, often dangling bait specifically modified based on the patterns and content of individuals' Internet use.

Advertising needs an updated code of ethics that takes into account the vulnerability of users in virtual environments, just as traditional news organizations need guidelines that take into account the new world of instantaneous deadlines and the ability to provide an unfettered public forum with unlimited reader commentary. But, unlike the twentieth century, when professional codes of ethics addressed all that was deemed important in mass communication, the twenty-first century demands a broader appreciation of ethical expectations for all producers and recipients of digital messages. It is impossible to stretch the standards codified for last century's print and broadcast news organizations to fit a virtual world of mass communication with its variety of message producers and distributors. Contemporary guidelines for mass communication ethics must address responsibilities of us all.

Communication is a powerful act and communicators are responsible for actions that follow from their messages. Those who receive the messages have responsibility as well. For example, if users are not offered sufficient information to allow them to accurately distinguish the kind of message that they are receiving, whether it is fact, opinion, fiction, or advertisement, for example, they can suffer harms by acting on mistaken beliefs. On the other hand, if citizens form mistaken beliefs because they avoid views that would make them uncomfortable with what they believe to be true, they are ethically culpable for actions or statements that they make based on willful ignorance.

As human beings, we are always limited by what we believe to be true. Forming true belief is a lifetime job. We have no choice but to act on the beliefs that we hold, but we also need to be open to new facts or new interpretations that can help us surrender beliefs that turn out to be false or incomplete.

Regardless of the communicator's chosen label or professional status, guidelines for contemporary mass communication should include the following:

1. recognition of power in the communicative act
2. accountability for the consequences of one's mass communications
3. the expectation that producers and distributors will do what they claim to be doing and
4. the expectation that producers and distributors will disclose ethically relevant information.

These guidelines hold regardless of whether a user identifies herself with a real name in the process of communication. The guidelines also hold for organizations, which means that social networking sites, such as Google+, should disclose their marketing interest in user data and provide justification for disclosure in requiring real names.

Democracy, as practiced online, can tolerate corporate capitalism in various forms including advertising and for-profit providers of information and opinion, just as it does in the physical world. But, the Internet has opened the mass communication field to allow for more active citizen participation than ever. As informed and critical citizens depend on active participation, requirements that favor corporate interests over individual expression should not be tolerated.

## REFERENCES

Google. (2011). *Your name and Google+ Profiles*. Retrieved October 12, 2011, from Google+: http://www.*Google*.com/support/plus/bin/answer.py?answer=1228271

Grohol, J. M. (2006, April 4). *Anonymity and Online Community: Identity Matters*. Retrieved March 13, 2012, from A List Apart: http://www.alistapart.com/articles/identitymatters/

Mill, J. S. (1869/1991). Of the Liberty of Thought and Discussion. In J. S. Mill, *Utilitarianism and Other Essays (ed J. Gray)*. New York: Oxford University Press.

Seigler, M. (2011, June 28). *Google+ Project: It's Social, It's Bold, It's Fun, And It Looks Good....Now For the Hard Part*. Retrieved October 12, 2011, from TechCrunch: http://techcrunch.com/2011/06/28/*Google*-plus/

Wikipedia. (2012, March 8). *List of acquisitions by Google*. Retrieved March 13, 2012, from Wikipedia: http://en.wikipedia.org/wiki/List_of_acquisitions_by_*Google*

Wikipedia. (2012, March 12). *List of Google Products*. Retrieved March 13, 2012, from Wikipedia, the free encyclopedia: http://en.wikipedia.org/wiki/List_of_*Google*_products

*II*

# Living an Authentic Life

## Chapter Three

# Social Media, Self-Deception, and Self-Respect

## Paul Bloomfield

Given that our topic is social media, it is perhaps a bit more apt than normal in philosophy to begin with an example from popular culture, in this case an episode of *Star Trek*. In "The Menagerie," Captain Kirk's predecessor Commander Pike is shown to be a badly scarred and disfigured quadriplegic whose only means of communicating is a light on the front of his wheelchair; one flash is "yes" and two are "no." (Perhaps they'd forgotten Morse code?) Anyway, Spock illegally hijacks the Enterprise to bring Pike to a forbidden planet called "Talos" on which beings with giant heads are able to project illusions in which people can live. Spock does this so Pike can live an illusory life out of his wheelchair and without his impairments. The rest of the details don't matter for our purposes; what is important is the seemingly righteousness of Spock's actions, despite the laws he breaks, because we pity Pike and are happy for him to be able to live on Talos, free from his dreadful real life and with at least the illusion of good health and fine well-being.

Our approval of the outcome runs afoul of the way most common-sense moralists frown at the idea of living under an illusion and the philosophical literature is full of thought experiments which we are supposed to pump up our intuitions about the importance of living in the real world. There is Robert Nozick's (1974) famous "experience machine" in which we may hook ourselves up to a machine that allows us to choose and program our lives so that everything seems to go just the way we'd like. It is supposed to be obvious how bankrupt such a "life" would be. More recently, Michael Lynch (2005) asks us to imagine two doors to walk through, each of which will lead to indistinguishable lives from the first person perspective, except that in one life all our relationships will be genuine and authentic while in the

29

other they would all be fake and dishonest, even though one would never find out. "Which door would we walk through?" he asks us, and he is right that the vast majority of us are not apathetic about our choice even though afterwards we'd never know the difference. It is important to most of us that we are not fools, even if we do not know that we are fools; it is important to most of us that our friends be true friends, our beloveds and spouses truly faithful, and that they not just give us virtual simulacrum of being such: We think the "reality/appearance" distinction is particularly important in our personal relationships and that the truth of these matters cuts deep.

And now, given the existence of a veritable virtual reality, and all the variety of social media that exist—Facebook and Twitter, Second Life, in which people live through avatars of their own devising, or the so-called "massively multiplayer online role playing games" (MMORPG) in which people play adventure games as fictional characters of their choosing—we are nowadays confronted with choices about whether we'd like to live our own lives or whether we'd like to create ourselves, cut from whole cloth, and live as our favorite fictional characters. If you've ever wanted to be the brave knight who kills the dragon and rescues the princess, now you can be. What are we to say? Should we shed our mortal coils, like Commander Pike, and virtually live the lives we have heretofore only dreamt of, or should we suck up the life we are born into, suffering through the bitterness that it can hold and savoring whatever sweetness we can?

## SELF-DECEPTION, SELF-RESPECT, AND HAPPINESS

The answers to these kinds of questions fall squarely within the purview of moral philosophy and in particular from thoughts concerning the nature of *self-deception*, *self-respect*, and *happiness*. So, first we need to get clear on how these concepts are to be understood. Self-deception has received a great deal of attention in the philosophical literature, given how it presents many epistemological and moral puzzles about how we can be so good at fooling ourselves about ourselves. Here, we may roughly follow the analysis of it given by Robert Audi (1997). A person is understood as self-deceptive with regard to the truth of a proposition given two conditions: (i) the person who asserts its truth also knows or has good reason to believe that it is false and (ii) simultaneously has a desire for the belief to be true where this desire explains why the reason to think it is false is not given its due credence or is ignored outright.[1] So, if one (consciously or unconsciously) recognizes that one has reason to disbelieve a proposition that one wants to believe, and as a result (consciously or unconsciously) ignores this evidence, then this constitutes self-deception about the truth of the proposition.

Unsurprisingly, self-respect has received even more attention from moral philosophers, much of it being based on the literature concerning respect, which is considered by many, at least since Kant, to be a (or even the) fundamental moral attitude. Perhaps the most important distinction is between what is known as "recognition" and "appraisal" respect, and the distinction may also be applied to self-respect as a species of respect.[2] The argument may be run through quickly with regard to self-respect, and while the full argument below would have to make more of this distinction than we can go into here, having it in the backs of our minds will help to sharpen the rough concept of self-respect we'll mostly be working with.

## RECOGNITION RESPECT AND SELF-RESPECT

Recognition respect and self-respect is the sort of respect involved when we see ourselves as worthy of a base line level of treatment due to the humanity (or perhaps the agency or rationality) that we share with other humans. This is founded on the fact that, ontologically, we are all of the same kind, and insofar as this is true, we are all equals and deserve to be treated as such. It is recognition respect that bars the moral legitimacy of slavery, or discrimination based on gender, race, etc.[3] People who lack recognition self-respect see themselves wrongly as inferior to others, while people who think too much of themselves fall prey to arrogance.[4] Importantly, when people lack proper recognition self-respect, this is based on the self-deceptive belief that they are fundamentally either worse or better than other human beings, as less or more worthy of this sort of respect than everyone else. So, in recognition respect, we do not need to earn it, rather we deserve it based on what kind of thing we are; in our case, we are human beings, members of Homo sapiens. In contrast, appraisal respect and self-respect is earned. It is a form of respect determined by how we evaluate others and ourselves based on life achievements or the quality of one's character. Colloquially, appraisal self-respect is close to self-esteem, and failures of it are correlated with over- or under-valuing what we have accomplished or failed to accomplish in our lives, or concern self-deceptive beliefs about the kinds of people we are, what our character strengths and weakness are. So, notice that someone with very, very low self-esteem might nevertheless insist on being given the same rights that others have, they might say, "However rotten I may be, I don't deserve to be treated like a slave."

The crucial fact about self-respect for our purposes is that there is an important sense in which we can be mistaken about whether or not we have it; it is not constituted by our subjective estimations. The objectivity involved can be seen by noting that self-respect requires that we respect our selves as we really are and not just as we wish we were or weren't.[5] Leaving aside inferiority and servility for the moment, I might easily engage in self-aggrandizing or arrogant behavior as a result of thinking that I am better in some ways than I truly am.[6] In this latter case, I might insist I have self-respect, as arrogant people tend to think of themselves as people of great self-respect. But if I adopt an attitude of respect to myself based on an image of who I wish I were but in fact am not, then my self-respect is fraudulent, regardless of whether or not I can see this. So, to bring together self-deception and self-respect: if I have self-deceptive beliefs about who I am and I base my attitudes toward myself on these false beliefs, then any self-respect which I think I accrue (or fail to accrue) as a result of these self-deceptive beliefs is fraudulent and not genuine self-respect.[7]

## LIVING A HAPPY LIFE

Finally, we come to happiness. Of course, this word has many legitimate meanings based on the variety of nouns that can be modified by the adjective "happy." Two important senses of it are demarcated by thinking first of being in a "happy mood" or having a "happy feeling," or some other affective mental state which may last a long or short amount of time. This sense of the term may be contrasted to another sense of it based on the idea of living a "happy life," referring by this to what the Greeks called "eudaimonia." Eudaimonia gets translated variously as either "flourishing," "well-being," or "happiness." "Happiness" in this sense is predicated over a person's life taken as a whole and denotes a life lived well, such that a person who is "happy" in this sense has lived excellently, or lived the proverbial "Good Life." We should not specify up front in any great detail what the Good Life looks like, for this would beg too many normative questions that should be settled only by a substantial debate. For now, we can rest with our intuitions that a "happy life" should represent the sort of life desired by people who respect themselves based on what they perceive as "best in life."

There is one way, however, in which this latter sense of "happiness" must be specified. This is the sense in which the best life is simply not the life where one is always in a "happy mood" or is experiencing "happy feelings." The "happy life" is not going to be subjectively constituted in the way "happy moods" or "happy feelings" are.[8] The reasons for this are many and complicated.[9] For example, we typically think that living the Good Life implies having integrity, which is not subjectively constituted, and having at least some concern for justice or fairness, and, these imply having genuine self-respect.[10] It is safe to assume that all parties to the debate will acknowledge up front that people cannot live happy lives if they are regularly disrespecting themselves, or if they lack self-respect. Perhaps someone would like to question this idea and defend the idea that a person can live a happy life without self-respect, but such a defense is hard to imagine and constitutes a large burden of proof to shoulder.[11] Common sense says that people who are living the Good Life or living the best lives possible respect themselves and indeed it is not unnatural to say that self-respect is more than merely instrumentally valuable for the Good Life but is actually partly constitutive of it.

## GENUINE SELF-RESPECT CANNOT BE HAD BY PRETENDING

Given all this background we are finally in a position to return to the issue of whether or not to live to some degree within virtual reality instead of real life. Remember the sorry case of Commander Pike. Pike was happy to live an illusory life since his real life offered him so very little. But compare this psychologically understandable fiction to the real life example of Christopher Reeves, the actor, who became paralyzed from the neck down at the age of 42. Reeves struggled mightily against his physical problems, and by all accounts exhibited extraordinary courage and fortitude in the face of horribly incredible adversity. I do not think it is a stretch to say that Reeves lived the best life anyone possible could, given the circumstances into which he found himself. Were a virtual life for him possible in which he could move around and have the sense of complete good health, it would certainly be understandable if he had chosen it, just as Pike's choice was understandable. But however more pleasant a virtual, fictional world might be in such cases, it would nevertheless not allow for the same sort of genuine self-respect that we have while struggling with the reality of the actual world. While the subjective feeling of Reeves' life might be more pleasant in a virtual world in which he was not paralyzed, there is an important sense in which any "happiness" and "self-respect" he would virtually have would be self-deceptively fraudulent: these attitudes would not be based on who or what his life actually is, but rather on a fantasy of how he wishes it were.

The important distinction here, by the way, is not between the virtual and the real but rather between pretending to be someone and actually being someone. If Reeves had access to a prosthetic robot through which he could virtually engage with the actual world, then this changes the story and the moral conclusions we should draw would have to be suitably modulated. The problem is in choosing to live in a fictional world where we may pretend that we are not who we actually are.

## VIRTUAL LIVES AND SELF-DECEPTION

These worries regarding self-deception come in when people start treating their virtual lives *as if* they were real. If I am playing some MMORPG and I'm going around killing dragons and casting spells and the like, none of this speaks to whether or not I am courageous and brave; rather, one might worry about actual cowardice as the cause of my retreat into the game. [12] And yet the worry is that players of games are thinking better of themselves, not as game players but as people, as a result of playing these games. The worry is that they may begin to build their self-conceptions on their virtual selves. [13] The issues are slightly different for other forms of social media like Second Life, Facebook, or Twitter, but they are no less real. To see the point with regard to Facebook, note simply that the vast majority of people do not present all of themselves on their Facebook page, but rather only the good or happy things that happen to them; they choose only flattering photos to post, write about accomplishments, or promotions, but do not reveal negative events in their lives in such a public forum, rarely do people post about events of which they are ashamed, of painful rejections they have experienced, of defeats they have suffered. [14] We might imagine confiding such sad realities to close friends in confidence, but not on Facebook. So, we ought not to fool ourselves into thinking that we are the people who we represent ourselves as being on Facebook; at best this is a shallow simulacrum. The point is that the difference between what is virtual and what is real, the appearance/reality distinction, is important insofar as our attitudes towards ourselves may be based on our ignoring the distinction or thinking that it doesn't matter.

Everyone may acknowledge that games are games and fun is fun and there's nothing intrinsically wrong with any of it. There is even nothing wrong with escaping from reality for a few hours now and then. [15] But it is likely there are reasons that people retreat into the computer; reasons why people do not want to be who they really are and why people seem to lie so much in chat rooms and websites. Reasons we can find on the internet, as Jeffrey Hancock (2007) writes, that "boys can be girls, the old can be young, ethnicity can be chosen, 15-year-olds can be stock analysts – and on the Internet no knows you're a dog." [16] Research seems to indicate that lying is more frequent in computer-mediated communication than in face-to-face communication (Walther, 2007). Research also seems to indicate that lying is most widespread in media that is synchronous, recordless, and distributed. [17] One reason is that it is easier to get away with lying or being someone else on-line than it is in real life, and research shows that highly motivated liars are harder to catch on-line than in real life: in real life, most of the time, the more motivated the liar, the higher the likelihood of detection, this is called "the motivational impairment effect," while Hancock et al. found the opposite in digital deception, a "motivational enhancement effect." [18]

## THE COURAGE TO LIVE OUR OWN LIVES

So, people deceive each other more on-line and tend to do so more success-fully. The further question is whether people are more likely to self-deceive on-line and there may be reason to think so. Virtual reality seems so desirable because it is so plastic, because we can allow ourselves, with a great deal of similitude, to act as if we are other than we in fact are and in so presenting ourselves to others successfully, we are likely to take such success to heart. If I am praised by others on-line for the ways in which I present myself and take pleasure in this, and the pleasure is actual, then I am to some degree more likely to come to think this pleasurable praise reflects something actual about me; the pleasure is actual despite being based on something which is importantly non-actual. And if we add to this a reason to be unhappy with real life, so that one desires more to be who one is on-line than who one really is, then all the pieces of self-deception are present. It would be "all too human" for us to allow the pleasure of on-line life to affect our self-concep-tion. And yet, sadly, all such effects are self-deceptive, all such effects render "self-respect" more fraudulent, and any "happiness" supposedly garnered from it that much less genuine. If successful deception of others is easier in a virtual world, then it is not unreasonable to think the same is true for self-deception: the more we pretend that we are not ourselves, the less we are actually living our real lives. And yet time goes on and our lives can become increasingly fictional, whether we realize this or not.

We must not be heartlessly unsympathetic to the reasons some escape to on-line life. Sometimes, in some cases, living to kill fake demons may be the best a person can do. People's lives can be shackled by introversion or loneliness or sadness; it may be extraordinarily painful for all sorts of reasons to interact with real people in the real world. For example, Aristotle said that people who are horribly ugly could not, for that reason alone, be happy, be eudaimon.[19] There may be good reason to think that he was not right about this, but if one were horribly disfigured, in an Elephant-man sort of way, so that people cringe and look away, or, even worse, stare and gawp and gawk, it is understandable that on-line interactions may be much easier and more pleasant. No one is to blame or be condemned for wanting to escape some debilitating problem. But what is essential to remember is that there is an important sense in which such escape is never for free and that living virtual-ly is always second best, always a step down, always second rate. It will only be morally chosen as a lesser of two evils, and even then what is lost is unrecoverable. If it is psychologically possible, it is far, far better to be truly courageous, just, temperate and wise in real life than merely appearing to be so on-line. The logic of morality alone may make it trivial to say that we should all do as much as we can to improve ourselves, our lives and our characters. But it may also be a substantial challenge to live with the courage and steadfastness to defeat our real-life demons, instead of only being strong enough to face them virtually.[20]

## NOTES

1. See also Audi (1986), McLaughlin and Rorty (1988), and Butler (1900) for a helpful classic text.

2. Darwall (1977), for a similar earlier treatment, see Telfer (1968).

3. For a further development of the moral implications of these ontological facts, see Bloomfield (2008).

4. Dillon (2004). For a classic treatment of servility, see Hill, Jr. (1973). See also work on the "impostor syndrome" in Kolligian and Sternberg (1990) and for psychologically supporting a negative self-image, see Snyder and Higgins (1997). For further helpful work on arrogance, see White Beck (1960) and Tiberius and Walker (1998).

5. I do not mean for the use of the noun "self" to imply some metaphysical entity which somehow is to stand independently of us, but is rather façon de parler to ease discussion of reflexive attitudes which the self may have toward itself.

6. Indeed, there is a sense in which arrogance involves a double self-deception that I will not go into here. See the article by Dillon (2004).

7. For more on how we can be wrong about these "reactive attitudes" see Bloomfield (2011).

8. It is practically a commonplace in contemporary debates about happiness and self-deception to point out that people who are honest with themselves about themselves are more likely to be depressed than those who engage in some healthy forms of self-deception. For a full and empirically informed refutation of this, see Badhwar (2008).

9. For a full-blown treatment of the errors of subjectivism in this regard, see Haybron (2008), especially chapters 10 and 11.

10. For a full treatment of this argument see Bloomfield (2011).

11. I think the only people who may not accept this assumption are those who accept a particularly flagrant and shameless form of hedonism that says that if the greatest pleasures were self-debasing that one ought to nevertheless pursue them.

12. I am happy to acknowledge the usefulness of virtual reality for learning such tasks as being a pilot or even perhaps a soldier. What I insist upon is that, however much virtual training one has, one is not a pilot until one has experience flying real planes; mutatis mutandis, one only has real courage when confronting real danger.

13. Cf. note 7.

14. I owe this idea to Walker (2011).

15. It is worth noting that the average player of MMORPGs is on-line 22 hours a week and 11% of players are on-line 35 hours a week. 50% of players consider themselves "addicted." Statistics are from *The Daedalus Project* (n.d.).

16. The reference in the quote is to *The New Yorker* cartoon, by Peter Steiner, from 5 July 1993.

17. Hancock (2007) p. 294. Strictly speaking, the internet is never "recordless," though accessing the records can be extraordinarily difficult, giving the illusion of there being no record. My thanks to Austen Clark for discussion on this point.

18. Hancock (2007) p. 298.

19. " . . . the man who is very ugly in appearance or ill-born or solitary and childless is not very likely to be happy, and perhaps a man would be still less likely if he had thoroughly bad children or friends or had lost good children or friends by death. As we said, then, happiness seems to need this sort of prosperity. . . . " Aristotle (1998).

20. An earlier draft of this paper was delivered at the University of Connecticut's Department of Philosophy, and I thank my colleagues there for helpful discussion. Helpful comments also came out of discussion at the University of North Florida's Symposium on Social Media and the Value of Truth, with special thanks to Mitchell Haney.

## REFERENCES

Aristotle (1998). W. D. Ross (trans.) *Nicomachean Ethics*, 1099b, W.D. Ross (trans.). Oxford: Oxford University Press.

Audi, R. (1997). Self-Deception, Rationalization, and the Ethics of Belief. In his *Moral Knowledge and Ethical Character*. New York: Oxford University Press.

Audi, R. (1986). Self-Deception and Rationality. In M. W. Martin (Ed.) *Self-Deception and Morality*. Lawrence: University Press of Kansas.

Badhwar, N. (2008). Is Realism Really Bad for You? A Realistic Response. In *Journal of Philosophy* 105 (2), 85-107.

Bloomfield, P. (2011). Justice as a Self-Regarding Virtue. In *Philosophy and Phenomenological Research*, 82 (1) 46-64.

Bloomfield, P. (2008). The Harm of Immorality. *Ratio*, XXI (3), 241-259.

Butler, J. (1900). Sermon X—Upon Self-Deceit. In J. H. Bernard (Ed.) *The Works of Bishop Butler, 2 vols.* London: MacMillan.

The Daedalus Project. (n.d.). The Psychology of MMORPGs, retrieved from http://www.nickyee.com/daedalus/.

Darwall, S. (1977). Two Kinds of Respect. *Ethics* 88 (1), 36–49.

Dillon, R. (2004). Kant on Arrogance and Self-Respect. In C. Calhoun (Ed.) *Setting the Moral Compass*. New York: Oxford University Press.

Haybron, D. (2008) *The Pursuit of Unhappiness*. New York: Oxford University Press.

Hancock, J. (2007). Digital deception: Why, when and how people lie online. In K. McKenna, T. Postmes, U. Reips & A.N. Joinson (eds.), *Oxford Handbook of Internet Psychology*. Oxford: Oxford University Press, 291.

Hill, Jr., T. (1973). Servility and Self-Respect. In *The Monist* 57 (1) 87-104.

Kolligian, Jr., J. and Sternberg, R. (Eds.) (1990). *Competence Considered*. New Haven: Yale University Press.

Lynch, M. (2005). *True to Life*. Cambridge: MIT Press.

McLaughlin, B., Rorty, A. O. (Eds.) (1988). *Perspectives on Self-Deception*. Berkeley: University of California Press.

Nozick, R. (1974). *Anarchy, State, Utopia*. New York, Basic Books.

Pineiro-Escoriaza, J. C. (dir.) (2008). *Second Skin*. documentary film.

Snyder, C.R., and R.L. Higgins. (1997). Reality Negotiation: Governing one's self and being governed by others. In *General Psychological Review* 1, 336-50.

Steiner, P. (1993). "No one knows you're a dog" cartoon. *The New Yorker Magazine* (July 5).

Telfer, E. (1968). Self-Respect. *Philosophical Quarterly* 18, 114–21.

Tiberius, V. and Walker, J. (1998). Arrogance. In *American Philosophical Quarterly* 35, 379–90.

Walker, R. (2011). Disliking the Facebook 'Dislike'. Retrieved from *Marketplace* American Public Media at http://www.marketplace.org/topics/disliking-facebook-dislike.

Walther, J. (2007). Selective self-presentation in computer-mediated communication: Hyperpersonal dimensions of technology, language, and cognition. In *Computers in Human Behavior* 23, 2538-2557.

White Beck, L. (1960). *A Commentary on Kant's Critique of Practical Reason*. Chicago: University of Chicago Press, p. 219–22.

*Chapter Four*

# Social Media, Speed, and Authentic Living

## Mitchell R. Haney

This is ultimately an essay in the ethics of living. As such, my concern is thoroughly normative in nature. In fact, it may even dabble in a bit of moralizing. In particular, I am curious about what is required for living-well by our own lights; particularly, in an age where the use of social media has become ubiquitous. I will warn the reader that the conclusion I urge here may be sobering for those who hold that the platforms of social media are personally liberating and who remain tantalized by the prospects of its value in the lives of people.

Polonius's final advice to Laertes was, "To thine own self be true." In the Elizabethan age this likely meant to be true to one's own best interests; especially, to avoid behavior that would be harmful to one's reputation (Guignon, 2004). It now has a more substantive interpretation that one should live a life which reflects our deepest concerns and commitments. It beckons us to personal integrity or authentic living of a certain kind—a personally valuable existence. I will contend that this goal requires time to discover what one most cares about and that the structurally imposed speed of social media appears to be antithetical to the importance of such time.

In the present age, the vast realm of social media from MMORPGS (Massively Multi-Player Online Role-Playing Games), such as World of Warcraft and Second Life, to the social networking media of Facebook, MySpace, Twitter and others, increasingly occupy people's attention and, for many, they hold these activities to be a part of what makes their lives satisfactory. A few philosophers have taken up the question of the value of these emerging technologies. Here I too will enter the fray.

Hubert Dreyfus is a philosopher who has long been skeptical of the value of electronic technology in our lives. In a recent work, he has raised concerns about the value of the internet especially as a social medium (Quoted in French, 2010). In particular, Dreyfus has proclaimed that one cannot find valuable living in the social media venue of Second Life. In Second Life you choose an avatar (a virtual self of your own creation) and lead your avatar to live out a life interacting with other avatars, including socializing, as well as purchasing products and services with which to "live," such as, clothing, real-estate, etc. Dreyfus argues that though one's avatar can mimic life in the real-world, it cannot be a life of authenticity. One may wonder why one would feel the urge to argue for this conclusion given that Second Life is by design illusory and artificial. The hours and dedication users of MMORPGs (including Second Life) give to developing their avatars in these virtual worlds make this a relevant question. A casual look at market studies appears to show that regular players average between 20 and 25 hours per week and avid players average 48 hours per week developing the lives of their avatars. Dreyfus argues that the virtual metaverse of Second Life allows us to deeply distract ourselves from the authentic life in which one is called to face up to one's finitude and the vulnerability of all one cares about (French, p. 103). In Dreyfus's mind, what makes the MMORPGs inauthentic and an impoverished mode of living is that they promote the denial of the human condition, in particular human suffering, finitude, impotence, and the moral indifference of the universe.

## SOCIAL MEDIA AND THE DEFINITION OF THE GOOD LIFE

Philosopher Peter French argues that Dreyfus's critique of Second Life relies upon a singular conception of the good life, which is itself clearly open to question. French rightfully queries, "Why should the criterion of (an authentic) life be bravely facing the truth of human finitude and the vulnerability to failure and the impermanence of all of our most treasured projects. . . ?"(French, p. 103). By way of contrast to Dreyfus's existential concerns about Second Life, French offers the story of a white male, Bob, who is a paralyzed and disfigured Iraq war veteran and who suffers from PTSD and a deep loneliness (French, p. 101–102). Bob hears about Second Life and decides to check it out. For no particular reason, he designs his avatar to be a beautiful African American woman with platinum blond hair. Bob's avatar, after months of regular and then avid playing, has a business, numerous friends, and a lesbian relationship in this virtual world. Bob spends most of his waking hours in Second Life, absorbed by the experiences of his avatar. French asks, is this man's second life less meaningful than his first simply in virtue of the fact that his avatar's experiences are virtual rather than real? French argues that Bob's life is not to be judged as impoverished on the basis of so narrow a conception of authentic living as proposed by Dreyfus. French argues, following Harry Frankfurt, that what makes a life meaningful is our seeing to the flourishing of the objects we care about. And Bob cares deeply about the welfare of his virtual self and mate in Second Life, and so finds meaning in his avatar's successes and failures. So, even in immersing ourselves in MMORPGS like Second Life, we may find objects over which we can experience significant joy and regret. As such, French concludes that one can lead an authentic life through the social medium of Second Life when we care deeply about our avatar's welfare and her projects.

I am not quite convinced that finding meaning and value in a world of virtual objects and projects can be considered as authentic as concern for those in the real world, because intuitively it seems to me that there is something about the illusory element of MMORPGs that makes them less valuable than caring about the welfare of real things and doings. (See Bloomfield in this volume for such an argument.) However, I am not quite sure how to make that case at this time without consequently disparaging other virtual worlds such as those found in novels, films, and theoretical physics, but the object of my concern lies elsewhere. I want to urge that the most popular forms of social media, Facebook and MySpace, do not lend themselves to even subjective well-being, that is, to developing and sustaining objects of genuine concern on which our sense of personal well-being depends.

## LIVING A LIFE WORTH LIVING

I think that French's use of Frankfurt's ideas from "The Importance of What We Care About" (Frankfurt, 1988) is on the right track as to how we should best understand authentic living or, at the very least, subjective well-being, e.g. what it is to flourish by our own lights. To live a life worth living from a personal point of view is to act in ways that reflect what we most truly care about, and the value of our living is measured both by how well we do this and how well the objects or projects about which we care fare in this world. The benefit of this view is that it allows for a plurality of authentic ways of living rather than those limited to one conception of the good life, like the dreary, existential one favored by Dreyfus.

Let us for a moment consider some of the details of Frankfurt's understanding of the importance of what we care about. The notion of caring about something is, in part, related to our behavior but it is broader than ethics. We can care about things other than being moral. (Although morality is often something we care about deeply.) We find, according to Frankfurt, that "more or less stable attitudinal and behavioral disposition(s)" in part reflect what a person cares about (p. 82). But there is more to it. To care about something is to be invested in it. It is to identify ourselves with our objects and projects about which we care and this makes us "vulnerable to losses and susceptible to benefits" (Frankfurt, 83) depending on how they make out in this world. To care about something is in part to find or to choose an affinity with that thing. A typical example of such caring is that of parents to their child. The child's interests are the parent's interests, because the parent is invested in the welfare of the child. And as the child's well-being is enhanced or decreased so is the well-being of the parent. Thus, parenting is often held out as a paragon of caring. However, this still is not all. There is a final characteristic to the Frankfurtian notion of care.

To care about something is more than just happening to believe that something is valuable or to want or to desire something to be the case. Believing, wanting and desiring can happen for just a moment, but to care about something requires an extended pattern of thinking, feeling, and imagining. It is a pattern of investment in an object of concern. A life of momentary likes and dislikes does not constitute an agent that cares about anything at all, because then cares would be indistinguishable from mere impulses, says Frankfurt (1988, p. 83-84) To care about something requires a persistence of attitude and behavior over time, as well as a pattern of appropriate emotional responses to how well one's object of care fares over that time. By way of continued example, parents that only cared for their child for a moment or even moment to moment but did not see their parenting as an extended investment of themselves, a continued meaningful project, would not be one who cares for their child; instead, such a parent would have a repeated want or desire rather than something they conceive as integral to who they are. We can more easily abandon our wants and desires than we can our cares, says Frankfurt (84), precisely because of the projected investment that is constitutive of cares and which we do not find in mere wants and desires.

In sum, according to Frankfurt, to care about something is to be invested in the welfare of an object over time and to have such a care guide one's attitudes and behaviors accordingly. For our purposes here, I propose that the person who is to have any possibility of subjective well-being must nurture attitudes and act and feel in ways which reflect what they most care about. And to have such objects of concern, whether they be people, principles, or states of affairs, takes time to experience life and to reflect on various objects of possible concern which life has to offer. In short, we must listen to ourselves so as to decide what to care about.

Returning now to social media. I am willing to grant, for now, that some social media, such as MMORPGs, might enable users to be true to what they care about. The medium of these games is such that over a period of time, an agent, like French's Bob, might come to care deeply about the welfare of his avatar and find his own subjective welfare rising or falling with her fortunes. However, MMORPGs are neither the only form of social media nor the most popular form.

## STRUCTURES OF SOCIAL MEDIA MAY PREVENT AUTHENTIC LIVING

Second Life and World of Warcraft boast a total of 34 million subscribers. By contrast, Facebook estimates 500 million active users, MySpace 100 million, and Twitter 175 million. As such, these other social media venues have between triple and 14 times the number of users in comparison to two of the most popular MMORPGs. However, the social interface of these venues is quite different than MMORPGs' and, as I will suggest, the interface structures of these social media may jeopardize caring in ways that may not be threatened so by MMORPGs (although I suspect that MMORPGs fail to contain fully worthy objects of care on other grounds).

In Facebook, MySpace, and Twitter you create a profile after which you are urged to make connections with others from your present, past, or with those who have mutual interests or associations. In Facebook, those with whom you become connected are called "friends." From there, you and other users are urged through both prompts and the Facebook culture to keep your friends updated as to what you are doing and thinking as well as to comment on what they are doing and thinking. For instance, at the top of your Facebook page, there is always the open dialogue box "What's on your mind?" Analogously, the entire mechanism for Twitter is to post to your network short messages, "tweets," about what you are thinking, doing, etc., and anyone subscribed to your account will receive your messages instantly. My concern hovers around to what extent interfaces, such as these, impede the kind of habits necessary for developing or sustaining cares to which we can be true, and on which our subjective well-being depends.

It must be acknowledged that the time expended in the most popular of these social media forums, Facebook, is significantly less than for the MMORPGs we considered above. The average user in January 2011 spent about 23 hours per month on Facebook. A year ago it was approximately 7 hours. So, the number of leisure hours dedicated to social networking is quickly gaining on the 88 hours per month for regular users of MMORPs like World of Warcraft. So, the very popularity of Facebook, MySpace, and Twitter as leisure activities demands our attention. And although the number of hours spent on social networking still pales to the 88 hours averaged in World of Warcraft, it may also be the very speediness of Facebook and

Twitter and others that, I will suggest, makes these venues more adverse to the development and continuation of authentic caring—even while demanding fewer hours be logged actively Facebooking or tweeting.

## TEXT BITES CREATE PEOPLE OF IMPULSE

In MMORPGs you are largely free to wander and experiment with interactions with others in a range of virtual venues of your own choosing. Twitter, Facebook, and to a lesser extent MySpace, corral users to certain kinds of interfaces. Facebook's "what's on your mind" dialogue box, and the "like" button (among other tools) urge us to respond to others' lives as well as our own with little more than text bites (hypertext versions of "sound bites") or finger clicks. In addition, it goads users to various games and surveys which are meant to keep the user and her friends clicking and returning often to check their "news feed." As a matter of armchair evidence, the depth of the interface—on the whole—appears pretty shallow. I certainly notice that users (even friends of mine with advanced degrees) seem moved to post the most hackneyed information about their lives. "Out to eat. Spaghetti or Lasagne?" "Nite, nite, sleep tight..." "Today is the first day of the rest of your life...?" "I have a Master's degree. Why can't I figure out the nuts to change my car battery?"

These are each updates on Facebook I received in a 72 hour period. But why so many banal postings? One could post quite potent and meaningful updates, but such would take time for both writer and reader. Not only do such postings take time, but such extended time does not seem to be the culture of social networking sites. Unless your message can be captured in few words it will either not be supported by the medium (as in Twitter where you have a 140 character limit) or your audience may simply post "tl;dr" (too long and did not read). And the reason that one may not take the time to engage in any depth of expression is that when your ideas, thoughts, feelings, etc., are posted they remain easily accessible on an update page for one or maybe two viewings if you have an active group of posting friends. Thus, the time spent to write a significant and meaningful post is often outweighed by the minimal impact it will have due to the structure of the medium. The point of the medium is to urge us to return often lest we miss some bit of important news, like what your friend finally chose to eat or that today really is the first day of the rest of your life, or—better yet—a novel meaningless post from a friend, but it does not readily support significantly nuanced interactions between friends.

Any medium that compresses the richness of human experience and reflection into quick, momentary, text bites or to the press of a hypertext link is a medium which because of its limited temporal existence urges us not to develop or sustain lasting concerns but rather to exist in the temporary and fluid realm of our immediate beliefs, attractions and repulsions. Such a medium seems to subvert our ability to be true to ourselves by encouraging us to be creatures of impulse rather than people who care. Cares require time to develop through experience, reflection, and seeing what it is like to live with the responsibility for caring about the welfare of an object or project (e.g. such as a friendship in the real world). Facebook, Twitter and other social media venues involve mechanisms which may be anathema to developing such essential cares.

Caring takes time, but "tweeting," "friending," and "liking" in the metaverse of social media are instantaneous. Instantaneousness may be the new opiate of the masses. And social media is but one more expression of the dope (Brabazon, 2007). If Frankfurt is correct, we cannot find life worth living if we do not care about something. However, to determine, to develop or even to sustain objects and projects toward which we may invest ourselves, about which our own existence comes to be interconnected and on which the value of our lives hangs together into a coherent pattern of thinking, feeling and acting, requires extended periods of time. It requires time for self-discovery or autonomous choice. We need to experience life, reflect on the quality of our experiences, compare experiences, and judge what it is that we want to protect and pursue in our lives.

However, the extended periods of time necessary to listen to ourselves are not on offer in the most popular forms of social media. For instance, if I wait to reflect on a friend's post or tweet before I comment, it will quickly be old news and disappear from their update page or be lost in a whirl of novel, abbreviated postings. If I want to tweet a profound experience, I best be able to explicate it in 140 characters or less or it cannot be shared. In short, the most popular and growing social media venues lend themselves only to the entertainment of momentary impulses rather than in the development of cares through listening to oneself. But, as was said earlier, impulses cannot serve as a ground of subjective well-being, because impulses are fleeting and being true to oneself requires the extended commitments associated with caring about objects and projects in our lives. And, yet, ours is a culture that is ever increasingly coming to value and invest itself more and more in each individual having a presence in the metaverse of social networking. This does not bode well for human flourishing.

In fact, Hubert Dreyfus, in a different work, argues that the internet—in general—is structured altogether in such a way as to short-circuit our ability to develop genuine and lasting commitments (Dreyfus, 2001). Using Kierkegaard, Dreyfus argues that the internet's deep neutrality, e.g. the fact that nearly anything can be uploaded and treated with equal value, causes a great "leveling" of importance. All links on the internet are equal, according to Dreyfus, and this form of egalitarianism makes it difficult, if not improbable, for users to develop genuine commitments to things in a world that does not present itself as having objects more or less worthy of our attentions. Thus, it follows for Dreyfus that in the world of the internet Push-Pin truly is as good as poetry. As such, I am not the first to worry about the internet's inability to aid humans in their need to have objects and projects of care. However, my concern is about its speed subverting our ability to care rather than its value neutrality (although I am moved to believe that dimension of the internet is problematic as well).

## MUCH ADO ABOUT NOTHING?

Critics may protest the account on offer here either makes much ado about nothing or states the obvious. It may be claimed that I make too much of nothing, because the lack of depth of conversation on social networking sites is really no different than the mundane nature of ordinary face-to-face conversation. Our real-time conversations with others reflect mostly meaningless content as well. It may also be said that I am stating the obvious, because of course it is the case that social networking cannot be the basis of discovering proper objects and projects of care, but it can be used to help sustain the things we care about and discover in the material world as we find it. Let me take each of these criticisms in turn.

It is true that much ordinary conversation is relatively cursory and lacks much meaning and value to its interlocutors in and of itself. However, ordinary conversation is not structurally stilted (nor is ordinary writing for that matter) to favor only the cursory and fleeting in the way that social media are so structured. We can easily shift course in ordinary conversation to express and explore more deeply held objects of concern when time permits. Our speaking and writing is not artificially restricted by word count, etc., such that we can explore a range of ideas from the mundane to the most profound. In contrast, social networking interfaces have word and time limits that structurally and artificially truncate our conversations. Thus, social media's mechanics and culture promote shallow over deep understanding between those linked in its space. As such, it—by design—limits our ability to explore what we should really care about in favor of immediately present desires.

Even if we admit that genuine objects of care cannot be discovered in the metaverse of social networking, opponents will say that it can still be the case that it aids us in sustaining objects of care which are discovered or chosen in the experience of real life. Many report that they like the fact that social media enable them to maintain relationships in ways that they could not easily do otherwise, e.g. due to time or distance (Ellison et al., 2007). However, there are concerns about social media increasing teen risk-taking behavior due to the fact that social media allow for a certain measure of anonymity from other users which in turn mitigates the level at which they can be held responsible for their behavior, and it appears that it may extend adolescent narcissism. As such, the medium may pose a risk to developing mature caring about civility and friendship (LaPorta, 2009). And, there is a concern, called the "internet paradox," in which newly connected users find that they distance themselves from their family and friends, and subsequently are more depressed, in spite of the fact that the connectivity of social media is meant to bring people closer together (Kraut et al., 1998). Now, the results of research on the internet paradox are mixed. Some indicate the results mentioned above, and others show that users overcome this initial downturn in their own well-being and return to a state where they reconnect with objects of care like family and friends after the novelty of social media wears off (Kraut et al., 2002). However, one constant of the research is that significant numbers of users in long term studies report increased levels of stress. I surmise that stress arises because of juggling too many expectations between real and virtual relationships. As such, it appears that engagement with social media may not aid entirely in sustaining objects of care, such as interpersonal relationships in a life without unnecessary stress.

Connected to this criticism, the critic may ask, "Well what about the success of social media in something like the Arab Spring?" Did not the populace make good use of social media to express their deepest concerns about Arab leaders? In something like the Arab Spring, people did mine the resource of social media to express and nurture their object of care. However, note that they did not discover this object in virtual space, but in the material conditions of the real world. And, these people lived in a context in which due to a lack of options in the real world, they both discovered their object of care (e.g. greater freedom) as well as were moved to social media as a venue through which to care about their object (due to the lack of freedom to express their discontents openly). In the context of the western liberal world, it seems that people who have the privilege to access the internet generally have options galore. In fact, they may have too many options (Haybron, 2008). Thus, following Dreyfus, the world of social media in such a context just adds more value neutral options to the mix of all the possible objects and projects that one could value or pursue, but none stand out as more important than anything else. And, we are driven, via the speed of social media, to merely express our most present desires and whims rather than to reflect upon that which we care about most.

The nexus of the difficulties posed by social networking, I contend, is the pace or speed of the interactions. It is the instantaneous nature of social media which threatens to thwart our capacities to reflect and to choose by rewarding the impulsive and the merely casual. And it is through reflecting on our lived experience and choosing some projects or objects of importance, i.e. listening to oneself, that we can really be true to ourselves. And, being true to ourselves is a condition for the possibility of finding our own lives worth living. However, at this juncture, a bit more should be said about the nature and value of discovering that which one most cares about.

## THE ADJUNCTIVE VALUE

The process of discovery of our cares is best interpreted as an "adjunctive" value or virtue rather than a substantive or core value. An adjunctive virtue, according to Robert Audi and Patrick Murphy (2006), is a virtue that is not sought for its own sake and can be implemented for good or ill, and as such it is not a core virtue or good. Instead, an adjunctive virtue is a catalyst for achieving core goods or enhances core goods in various ways. It is not a good-in-itself because conscientiousness may enable good or evil ends, for example, systematic discrimination. Nevertheless, conscientiousness most certainly acts as an indispensable support to anyone's goods. What might such an account of listening to oneself look like in individual lives?

We may begin to understand the supportive or adjunctive value of discovering or choosing one's cares by contrasting it with ways in which the impulsiveness of social media can be disruptive to the project of acquiring and sustaining objects of ultimate concern. If we place the expectation on persons that they complete a task in a short period of time, e.g. rush them, then they will not be able to sustain objects of their concern in ways that they would when they have time to reflect. For instance, as psychologists John Darley and Daniel Batson (1973) discovered, even the presumably morally best of us will act contrary to easily fulfilled moral duties when pressed for time. In a series of experiments on the likelihood that people will act as good Samaritans, Darley and Batson tested seminarians. Some subjects were made to rush, and some were not, in order to give either a sermon on the parable of the Good Samaritan or on job opportunities in the clergy. Of those being rushed to deliver their talk, 90% of these seminarians failed to stop and aid a person that was obviously in need of help, regardless of whether or not they were sent to speak on the Good Samaritan or job opportunities.

Darley and Batson's work indicates that even the ability to meet the demands of common decency will suffer under time constraints, and common decency is but one common object of care (especially, one would think, among seminarians). Hence, there is some body of evidence for the claim that to impose a need for the instantaneous or the speedy and the merely casual may cause us to sacrifice objects or projects of personal importance, such as, helping others in need or personal principles. On the other hand, if people were to come to know the ways in which the pace of social media may contribute to sacrificing objects of their concern then might it be that more people would find the social media life less satisfying?

Another dimension that arises, even from one reading of the Darley and Batson experiment, (and one might read this into Millgram's infamous authority experiments as well) is that many people find the expectations of others translating into strong internal motivations to act and which are difficult to escape. As such, it appears that many people's sense of being rushed is likely a well-conditioned internalization of the motivational force of meeting others' expectations (especially those in positions of power or those who the agent values). In such a scenario, it is the case that people's freedom is curtailed and social media are structured, as I said above, to urge us to quickly respond to others' posts and to post regularly about ourselves.

If people's sense of self-determination is sacrificed to the expectations of a medium which urges in us an impulsive need to visit it often and to respond quickly and pithily to the posts of others, then part of the value of self-discovery of what one cares about is that it enables people's sense of self-determination. So, any account of such self-reflection, should acknowledge the importance of people's freedom to take their time in considering what they want to care about. So, the process of such self-discovery may be thought of as an adjunctive value to the value of personal freedom, in addition to contributing directly to living a life we find personally worthwhile.

## OBJECTS AND PROJECTS OF GENUINE CONCERN

I have urged that social media, at least in the guise of social networking sites, truncates our ability to find and sustain objects and projects of genuine concern. And, I have also urged that it is the speed which these media impose on us that is the cause the truncation. The imperative to be instantaneous and concise which, I suggest, is the heart of social networking interfaces, interferes with our ability to listen to ourselves and to discover what we care about. And without objects and projects to which we are personally committed we cannot be true to ourselves and to find a life which is fulfilling by our own lights. In conclusion, I want to suggest that these reflections urge us to use our leisure time, at least some of such time, in certain kinds of ways. One way is negative and the other positive.

First, and foremost, we should concern ourselves with the fact that users of social media are now averaging 23 hours per month on social networking. This is the equivalent of a part-time job, but presumably it is a use of our leisure time (even if it's on a break from work). And the reflections above advise that we ought to refrain from filling our leisure time solely with the sort of instantaneous activities which appear to be conducive to our projects and concerns but really aren't. In the same manner as many warn against filling one's leisure time with distractions of the television, the ruminations above warn us to not be fooled into thinking that social media aids us in discovering how to be true to ourselves. This normative warning should come as no surprise, because anything which consumes all our leisure time is likely to be vicious rather than virtuous. However, we should also take care not to be hoodwinked into thinking that our time spent in social media is anything much deeper than the instantaneous gratification found in many other passive forms of entertainment like television. For the speed of social media, like the passiveness of watching television, truncates our ability to come to care about the welfare of objects and projects in our lives.

Second, and much more positively, we should guard some of our spare time for more productive forms of leisure. An example of such may be what Annette Holba (2010) calls, "philosophical leisure." Holba builds an account of philosophical leisure, from both the history of the value of leisure and the phenomenology of our experience of it, in order to recall a "productive quiet" from the noise of "recreation" or entertainment. And, this "productive quiet" is either synonymous with or is the ground for self-discovery of which I wrote above. A part of our leisure time should be devoted to ruminating about that to which we are ultimately devoted or committed, and how the things for which we care ought to guide our behavior, as well as how these objects and projects contribute to who we are. As was urged above, in order to lead a fulfilling life by our own lights, we must have projects and objects about which we ultimately care. But, such things do not come to self-conscious commitment without attentive reflection. And some use of leisure should be aimed at that project, which I take to be part of Holba's defense of philosophical leisure. In short, without this use of some of our leisure time, we may lack the ability to be genuinely true to ourselves, which is one nexus in leading a fulfilling life.

## NOTE

An earlier version of this paper, "Social Media, Speed and Listening to Oneself," appeared in the journal *Listening: Journal of Communication Ethics, Religion, and Culture*, Vol. 46, No. 1, Winter 2011. 37-51.

## REFERENCES

Audi, R. & Murphy, P. (2006). The Many Faces of Integrity. *Business Ethics Quarterly,* 16 (1), 3-21.

Blizzard Entertainment (2011). us.blizzard.com/en-us/company/pressreleases.html?101007. Retrieved from www.blizzard.com

Brabazon, T. (2007, August 31). Come Back Karl. All is Forgiven. artsHub.co.uk/The UK Arts Portal. Retrieved December 6, 2010: http://www.artshub.co.uk/uk/newprint.asp?s...

Darley, J.M. & Batson, D. (1973). "'From Jerusalem to Jericho:' A Study of Situational and Dispositional Variables in Helping Behavior." *Social Psychology*, 27, 100-108.

Dreyfus, H (2001). *On the Internet*. New York, NY: Routledge.

Ellison, N., Steinfield, C., & Lamp, C. (2007). The Benefits of Facebook "Friends:" Social Capital and College Students' Use of Online Social Network Sites. *Journal of Computer-Mediated Communication*, 12, 1143-1168.

Facebook (2011) www.facebook.com/home.php?ref=home#!/press/info.php?factsheet. Retrieved from www.facebook.com.

Frankfurt, H. (1988) The Importance of What We Care About. In *The Importance of What We Care About: Philosophical Essays*. 80-94. Cambridge, UK: Cambridge University Press.

French, P. (2010) Worthwhile Living in *Second Life*. In *The Value of Time and Leisure in a World of Work*. Haney, M.R. & Kline, A.D. (eds), 101-115. Lanham, MD: Lexington Books.

Guignon, C. (2004) *On Being Authentic*. New York, NY: Routledge

Haybron, D. (2008) *The Pursuit of Unhappiness: The Elusive Psychology of Well-Being*. New York, NY: Oxford University Press

Holba, A (2010) The Question of Philosophical Leisure: A Philosophy of Communication. In *The Value of Time and Leisure in a World of Work*. Haney, M.R. & Kline, A.D. (eds), 39-57. Lanham, MD: Lexington Books.

Kraut, R., Kiesler, S., Boneva, B., Cummings, J., Helgeson, V., Crawford, A. (2002). Internet Paradox Revisited. *Journal of Social Issues*, 58 (1), 49-74.

Kraut, R., Patterson, M., Lundmark, V., Kiesler, S., Mukophadhyay, T., et al. (1998). Internet Paradox: A Social Technology that Reduces Social Involvement and Psychological Well-Being. *American Psychologist*, 53(9), 1017-1031.

LaPorta, L. (2009, October 28) . Twitter and YouTube: Unexpected Consequences of the Self-Esteem Movement? *Psychiatric Times*, 26 (11), 1-6.

MySpace (2011). myspace.com/pressroom/fact-sheet. Retrieved from www.myspace.com.

Secondlife (2011). secondlife.com/xmlhttp/secondlife.php. Retrieved from http://secondlife.com.

The Daedalus Project: The Psychology of MMORPGs (2011). www.nickyee.com/daedalus/archives/000891.php. Retrieved from www.nickyee.com/daedalus/

Twitter (2011). twitter.com/about. Retrieved from http://twitter.com.

*Chapter Five*

# Gossip in the Digital Age

## Vance Ricks

### INTRODUCTION

Gossip is both a source of deep pleasure and of deep anxiety, touching on our beliefs and feelings about exposure, reputation, and control. It is something that many people do and that very few people feel comfortable engaging in, at least not without a lot of rationalizing. In this chapter, I examine gossip "in general" before arguing that in an era of widespread online connectivity, we may need to rethink both the nature and the possible consequences of gossip. I make a few presumptions: that gossip in-itself is normatively loaded but morally neutral; and that in a digital age characterized by nearly at-will online connectivity and interaction, discerning between good and bad gossip might be more difficult.

My discussion proceeds in a few stages. I'll first explain why gossip might be philosophically interesting. Next, I'll clarify and defend the two presumptions listed above, by examining some of the possible social and political consequences of gossip in societies like ours, where the use of online technologies is increasing and increasingly ubiquitous. I'll also explore how the meaning of gossip itself might be affected by those technologies.

### CHARACTERIZING GOSSIP: SOME BASICS

Several features make gossip an interesting and important topic of philosophical reflection. Gossip is of *conceptual* interest. For instance: is the concept of gossip inherently negative, or is it possible to give a neutral or even positive characterization of it? Gossip is also of *epistemological* interest: it raises questions about testimony, about epistemic norms, and about the social dimensions of our knowledge. Gossip is, of course, of *ethical* interest, raising questions about virtues, motives, responsibilities, benefits, and harms. And gossip is of *political* interest: gossip is sometimes a way for social actors and institutions to assert, resist, or strengthen various social norms or political ideologies.

Gossip might also be interesting in other philosophical ways and for other philosophical reasons. In fact, it probably is. But that quick sketch ought to be enough to illustrate the ways in which an everyday social practice is not, for all that, trivial. As the discussion proceeds, I will examine each of those areas of philosophical interest. Let's begin with the conceptual area, with an attempt to clarify the central term. What *is* gossip?

It's hard to set out the necessary and sufficient conditions for something's counting as (an act of) gossip, and perhaps setting out necessary and sufficient conditions isn't a useful plan in the first place. It may be more fruitful, for this discussion, to follow others who have explored the subject, and offer a "prototypical" account of gossip (See Goodman and Ben-Ze'ev, 1994). This is meant to present elements that are typical of, but maybe not necessary for, something's being gossip. The prototypical account represents an amalgam of accounts from sociological, psychological, and philosophical literatures (See Dunbar, 1998; "Rumor and Gossip," and Bok, 1989 respectively). That prototypical characterization looks like this:

> Gossip is a particular type of conversation between at least two people, about at least one other person who is absent. The topic of the conversation is often, but not always, "personal" information (or facts) about that absent person.

That characterization needs to be supplemented, because it leaves out some important details. For instance, it leaves out important information about the speakers and about what the speakers are doing in having that conversation in the first place: about, for instance, the speakers' intentions. One aspect of speaker intention is related to the speakers' roles, relative to the person being talked about. To see this, think about two physicians who are comparing notes about a patient they have in common. Suppose that they're discussing the patient's progress or prognosis, with the aim of coordinating their treatment plans or their ability to respond caringly to their patient's anxieties. To the degree that the physicians are talking about her in their roles *as physicians*, it seems odd to say they are gossiping about her, even though the information they're discussing about that patient is quite personal. Another aspect of speaker intention is related to the speakers' motives. And here we face several challenges, not just because of the diversity of motives but also because of the ones that many writers about gossip have suggested are inherent to it.

I believe that gossip is a morally neutral concept. Unlike the concept of murder, where the notion of "unjustified" is an inseparable part of the concept, the *concept* of gossip doesn't seem to be that tightly joined to the notion of "bad or vicious motives." That view is not necessarily the majority one (Bok, pp. 89-91). Many social critics, going back to and including King Solomon (Ecclesiastes, 10:11-10:15), have described gossip as conversations that are motivated entirely, or significantly, by unworthy considerations and emotions: schadenfreude, pettiness, arrogance, or envy at worst; shallowness, boredom, or frivolity at best.

Any honest attempt to give a "prototypical" characterization of gossip will have to acknowledge that many *typical* cases of gossip seem to be motivated at least partly in those ways. However, it's important to leave open the possibility that those motives are not *inherent* to making gossip gossip. First of all, we do many things for a combination of motives only some of which might pass ethical muster. Second, it seems possible that something could be an occasion of gossip yet be motivated (mostly) by neutral or even positive considerations or emotions.[1] Third, and fundamentally, equating gossip with frivolous motives is mistaken; the *content* of gossip differs from the manner in which it's discussed. People can gossip about serious subjects in a serious way *or* in a frivolous way, and for (a combination of) serious *and* frivolous motives.

However, though it be morally neutral, the concept of gossip does seem to be *normatively loaded*. In other words: however "idle," or "empty," gossip might sound to other people, it typically centers on some sort of evaluation of some aspect of the person being gossiped about. There are all kinds of aspects of ourselves and others that we evaluate with reference to various norms, and there's a rich variety of evaluative criteria that we use to do it.

In their respective treatments of the subject, Margaret Holland (1996), Sisela Bok (1989), and Ronald DeSousa (1994) all independently suggest that a hallmark of gossip is its focus on some way in which the subject "is viewed as failing to live up to the (assumed to be) relevant standards"(Holland, p. 198). I agree with a different account, given by Laurence Thomas (1994), that it seems odd to describe cases where people are praising someone who is successfully living up to some standard as cases of gossip about that person. Still, treating those cases as cases of gossip would only provide *more* support for the idea that the concept of gossip is deeply connected to that of evaluation. But a goal—pointing out some way in which a person is (or isn't) measuring up to some standard or other—is not the same as a motive (e.g., to be cruel, to entertain oneself or one's interlocutor, to make oneself feel superior to someone else). Also notice that evaluative criteria include moral ones, but aren't limited to them: you can gossip about someone's musical taste; their ability to give a non-superficial keynote talk; their baseball skills; or their Sociology quiz results, none of which necessarily has a moral dimension.

A final addition helps to distinguish gossip from rumor mongering, if we need to do so. Prototypical gossip involves information that the imparter believes to be true, and where that belief plays an important role in motivating the conversation in the first place. When there's a conversation about information whose truth is unknown to, or a matter of indifference to, the speakers, then it seems more accurate to say that they're trading rumors. But the distinction, as we'll see below, might be difficult to maintain.

## CHARACTERIZING GOSSIPING: SOME BASICS

In the previous section, I claimed, gossip *as a concept* can be morally neutral: that it is not *necessarily* best understood in terms of suspect motives. I'll now discuss a way in which gossip *as an activity* can be morally neutral.

One way to try to say something interesting about gossip is to enumerate the ways in which gossip can serve both harmful and helpful ends and can be motivated by both vicious and neutral (or even virtuous) feelings. Then the "sides" are tallied up, and a judgment is rendered about gossip as a moral phenomenon. For example: those attracted to rights-based ethical frameworks might look askance at most gossip on the grounds that it violates others' legitimate expectations about what information is appropriately confidential, about who is entitled to disclose that information, or about who is entitled to form opinions using that information. Those using a benefits-versus harms-based framework could criticize gossip for its potential to damage relationships, harm reputations, and fundamentally, to hurt people's feelings. Virtue-based frameworks, meanwhile, would likely highlight some of the troubling vices that we associate with gossip: pettiness, schadenfreude, and nosiness.

Whatever the advantages to that overall approach, Emrys Westacott (2010) provides an appealing alternative way to proceed with a moral analysis of gossip. Westacott, whose approach is congruent with that of Bok (1989, pp. 94-99), suggests that our views of the moral features of gossip depend on our *prior*, and more general, views about the moral features of talking about another person, period. For instance, if we already think that it's generally wrong to violate someone else's confidence, or we already think that it's generally wrong to recklessly divulge information without concern for its effects, then we don't gain very much by calling those things "gossip" and condemning them on *that* basis. It isn't that they are bits of gossip and therefore morally suspect. Rather, it's the fact that they're examples of morally suspect behavior that makes those forms of gossip morally problematic. The advantage of that approach is that it again leaves open the possibility that there can indeed be morally neutral, or even morally beneficial, ways of gossiping. And therefore, that approach can lead to a less question-begging conversation about the ethical *and other* features of gossip.

For example, it's a commonplace among social scientists that gossip—because of its normative richness—can have important interpersonal and societal benefits (Beersma and Van Kleef, 2011). Gossip can provide ways to display and enhance one's social position. Though it can damage bonds between people, it can also help to create, strengthen, and repair bonds between people. It can be a way for people to learn more about each other, and thus—in an ideal case—play a role in helping us to recognize our common humanity (Dunbar, 1998). One dimension that anthropologists and sociologists have explored in some detail is the way in which gossip can actually help to *reduce* interpersonal conflicts (at least, in the short run) by providing a more indirect, less confrontational, way for one person to express negative attitudes about another person. And one of the bedrock elements of gossip—which is implied by the earlier characterization of it—is that because it's normatively loaded, it can serve the important social function of helping both to illustrate and to uphold various societal values.

But the fact that gossip can play that important social function is *itself* morally neutral. Illustrating and upholding societal values is good only to the extent that those values themselves are good ones. And on that point, there are two general and opposing emphases.

The first sees gossip, inasmuch as it plays that "policing" function, as primarily a conservative practice whose overall effect is, as John Stuart Mill suggests, to perpetuate what he calls, "the despotism of custom" (1869, paragraph 17). From that standpoint, gossip is closely linked to a readiness to hammer down the nail that sticks up in any of the myriad dimensions among which someone might try to distinguish themselves from others (Giardini and Conte, 2012). It's reflective of a desire to punish, even if "only" in the form of *tsk-tsk*ing, behaviors or beliefs that might challenge or threaten some aspect of the status quo. And at its worst, it's driven by a pathetic need to elevate the "normal" or respectable gossiper—at least in their own mind—over the weird, pathetic, or silly person who's being gossiped about (for an extended example see Sulzberger, 2011).

By contrast, the second emphasis acknowledges gossip's policing function, but instead focuses on the subversive use of that function. From that viewpoint, gossip allows a democratic sort of participation and presence in a society that is difficult if not impossible to achieve by other means. For instance, DeSousa—endorsing a perspective articulated by Louise Collins—writes, "[T]he cultural values articulated by gossip are not necessarily those of the dominant culture. On the contrary, they are at least as likely to be those of a subculture of the oppressed or at least of the less powerful. In this way, then, gossip could serve to articulate an alternative moral psychology as much as it might consolidate the dominant one." (1994, 28) We can see that phenomenon at work any place that those with relatively less power gossip about those with relatively greater power: hourly employees vis-à-vis salaried ones, or students vis-à-vis faculty, for example.

So far, I have not discussed the spaces in which the activity of gossip occurs. In many parts of this society, our conversations are mediated through digital technologies: phones, web sites, chat rooms, and gaming consoles, to take but a few examples. And while gossip has always been mediated through other, earlier technologies—writing comes to mind—it is worth asking about whether and how our currently dominant communications technologies might affect our thoughts about gossip, our practices of gossiping, and our evaluations of those practices. In the next section, I will investigate that topic by focusing on three characteristics of our "digital age": the hypertrophic attention economy; the resultant blurring of lines between "public" and "private" figures; and the ubiquity of data gathering and propagation. Each of these characteristics raises questions about the adequacy of the earlier characterization of gossip.

## GOSSIP AND GOSSIPING IN A DIGITAL AGE

There are a few implications of technologies that enable at-will online connectivity and interaction that raise interesting and important questions for how we understand gossip. There is the phenomenon of *hypertrophic attention economies*. There are the phenomena of *context collapse* and the push for *radical transparency*. And there is the *semi-intentional propagation* of personal information, made easier by many-to-many forms of communication (in other words, communications between several people *to* several other people, as in a comments page on someone's blog, or in a video chat room). What implications do those phenomena have for our gossip-related thoughts and practices?

By *hypertrophic attention economies*, I mean one outcome of the fact that some people who use digital tools experience a sort of "information overload," in which they feel overwhelmed—if not actively assaulted—by a barrage of notifications and information that arrives in their inboxes, in their web-based accounts, and on their phones. Information overload isn't a new phenomenon, of course, but it is perhaps true that for people who use digital tools, that sort of overload has reached unprecedented levels. Those users, like all sufferers of information overload, must either continue feeling overwhelmed, or they must prioritize what they'll pay attention to and what they'll ignore. In other words, the effect of information overload is to make *getting and keeping people's attention* a primary goal of our use of digital tools. Texts, photos, or sounds that are not sufficiently interesting or compelling will be ignored, or viewed for only a few seconds, or (worst of all) not forwarded to other people in order to compete for *their* attention. In a conversation about gossip, this feature of digital life should encourage us to ask the question, is it possible to gossip about oneself?

One reason to think so is the fact that more of us online are (voluntarily) saying and revealing more about ourselves, to more people in more places, than has ever been possible. That fact *alone* doesn't have implications for the concept of gossip—people have always talked about themselves at least as often as they have about others. However, one feature of life in a hypertrophic attention economy is that participants are engaged (again, not unprecedentedly, but to a new degree) in increasingly finely-grained forms of self-curation and self-presentation. The effort that we put into our online presences and personae can reflect any number of motives and wishes, but among those motives and wishes are desires for others' attention. Because that's true, it's possible to treat oneself *as* a sort of absent party: that is, as one whose own actions or preferences are presented for others' discussion[2]—be that on one's own social network site page, or in someone's information stream, or on someone else's blogs.

A closely related phenomenon is that of *context collapse*, connected to the idea of *radical transparency*. Context collapse is what occurs when the already-flexible boundaries between our social contexts are removed or weakened. In an online environment, contexts collapse when, for instance, status updates on a social network site are visible both by one's coworkers and by one's childhood friends, and where the context of those updates is erased. Information that is "appropriate" when directed at one audience is also viewed by audiences for whom it wasn't intended and for whom it might not be appropriate. Radical transparency is the desired goal for some who believe that the idea of separate contexts, inasmuch as it identifies "not disclosing" with "hiding" and "hiding" with "shame," is itself the problem—that if we were able and willing to present the same "face" to all of our social relations, then no one would be able to harm anyone else *merely by disclosing information about that person*, because that information would already be considered publically available. Context collapse and radical transparency raise deep questions about differential power and status; about the meanings and value of privacy-related concerns; and about notions of selfhood and authenticity (Boyd, 2012 & Solove, 2008, especially chapter 3). For this discussion, however, we should focus on a different concern about who counts as a "public" figure.

Nothing in the earlier characterization of gossip suggests that its status depends on its "targets." Nonetheless, I suspect that many people believe that there is an important difference between gossiping about one's next-door neighbor's life and gossiping about a nationally-known politician's or performer's life. That is to say (and US Supreme Court decisions have asserted), there are people who—by virtue of their roles or their circumstances—are visible to many other people, and there are other people who are more "obscure." And as a result, details about their lives and activities are open to scrutiny and discussion by the rest of us, in ways that do not apply to the details of more "obscure" lives.

But obscurity is at least partly a matter of where people's attention is directed, and digital technologies permit us to direct our attention to places that may always have been intriguing but that were, until now, difficult to reach. The distinction between public and obscure has always been a matter of degree (if not also of accident). It seems to be one that is increasingly difficult to maintain. We are now in an era where any person with a phone is a potential paparazzo; where any person with access to a computer can create a site to present any aspects of self that they wish; in which any person with an account with a social network service can develop and cultivate an audience of arbitrary size; in which any person with an audience can persuade that audience to unearth previously inaccessible information. Rather than thinking of some people as "public" figures and others as "private," it is increasingly evident that we are all—whether by accident or by design—potential public figures, relative to one or more specific audiences. To be sure, there are still many people who have no desire to be famous, or even "Internet famous," and who take active measures to remain obscure to as many audiences as possible. However, there are now more challenges to keeping those audiences—and their knowledge of our doings—separate from each other.

By the *semi-intentional propagation* of personal information, I mean information about our whereabouts; social relationships; hobbies; online activities; political commitments; and other information that is communicated sometimes with our knowledge and consent, sometimes without it, and sometimes somewhere in between, because of the particular devices or software that we use. Consider software or devices that, for instance, display our physical location, or that announce when we have "connected" to someone else (e.g., befriending someone or adding someone to one's network of acquaintances), or that make it possible for us to tell a mass of undifferentiated "Others" which songs we're listening to.

Because our digital tools allow and also encourage many-to-many forms of communication, it is trivially easy for that sort of information to be distributed far and wide in a variety of ways. Some of that distribution occurs without our knowledge (maybe because of the design of the services or the devices, or because we users have misconfigured them, or both). Services that allow us to "check in" (to announce to various online audiences that we are in a particular location or participating in a particular event), or to tell a mass of undifferentiated "Others" that we're listening to a particular song, might be doing so because we specifically took those actions. But they might be configured to do so automatically. Or we might have configured them early on and then forgotten that we've done so, or forgotten how to reconfigure them. Furthermore, we might—again, to varying degrees—be unaware of who exactly is receiving that information, and thus unaware of who is making decisions or judgments on that basis. That sort of (quasi-)automatic announcing, now referred to as "frictionless sharing"(Ingram, 2011), raises the interesting possibility that our devices and services themselves are now capable of doing something that resembles gossiping about us. That is to say, those devices/services are able, to a greater or lesser degree independently of our control or wishes, to divulge our personal information to others. Certainly, that is how many users report experiencing the disclosure of that information: as intrusive, surprising, and sometimes upsetting as they report when the source is another human.[3]

## THE FUTURE OF GOSSIP: CONCLUDING REFLECTIONS

The sketch presented above shows some of the ways in which we can think about gossip, as well as new ways in which we might need to think about it, in the light of a reconfigured sociotechnical landscape. Fundamentally, however, gossip floats above that landscape. Gossip, its opportunities, and its risks will remain inextricably connected to the larger opportunities and risks of our living as social beings.

## NOTES

This paper is adapted and expanded from a talk that I gave at the 15th Annual University of North Florida Graduate Student Philosophy Conference in Jacksonville, Florida, in March 2012. My sincerest thanks go to Karla Pierce and Mitch Haney for arranging the invitation; to the audience for their comments and questions; and to Jessica Harper for her insights, encouragement, and support. I also thank Professor Sisela Bok, whose conversations with me about her groundbreaking book, *Secrets* (Vintage Press 1989), first led me to be interested in ways of extending her insightful and elegant treatment of gossip.

1. Imagine someone who—by his own admission—is an inveterate gossip, but whose gossip consists mostly of *good news* in his friends' lives that he is thrilled to divulge to his other friends because he wants everyone to be able to celebrate that news.

2. Bok, p. 93: "Though it is hard to gossip about oneself, one can . . . talk about one's doings that include others in such a way as to arouse gossip. Compare, from this point of view, the rumored divorce and the announced one."

3. But what about the *normative* dimension that I claimed is part of the practice—if not also the concept—of gossiping? Are digital devices and services engaging in some sort of normatively loaded activity by reporting that I "liked" a certain movie, that I purchased a certain item, or that I have increased my audience by another ten people?

# REFERENCES

Beersma, B., and G. A. Van Kleef. (2011) "How the Grapevine Keeps You in Line: Gossip Increases Contributions to the Group." *Social Psychological and Personality Science* 2, no. 6, 642-649.

Ben-Ze'ev, Aaron. (1994) "The Vindication of Gossip." In Goodman and Ben-Ze'ev, 11-24.

Bok, Sissela. (1989) *Secrets: On the Ethics of Concealment and Revelation.* 3rd ed. New York, NY: Vintage Books.

Boyd, Danah. (2012) "The Power of Fear in Networked Publics", http://www.danah.org/papers/talks/2012/SXSW2012.html accessed 10 March 2012.

Collins, Louise. (1994) "Gossip: A Feminist Defense". In Goodman and Ben-Ze'ev, 106-116.

DeSousa, Ronald. (1994) "In Praise of Gossip: Indiscretion As a Saintly Virtue." In Goodman and Ben-Ze'ev, 25-33.

Dunbar, Robin. (1998) *Grooming, Gossip, and the Evolution of Language.* Cambridge, MA: Harvard University Press.

Giardini, F., and R. Conte. (2011) "Gossip for Social Control in Natural and Artificial Societies." *Simulation* 88, no. 1, 18-32.

"Go Ahead. Gossip May Be Virtuous. - New York Times", n.d. http://www.nytimes.com/2002/08/10/arts/go-ahead-gossip-may-be-virtuous.html?pagewanted=all&src=pm, accessed 01 May 2012

Goodman, Robert F. and Ben-Ze'ev, Aaron. (1994) *Good Gossip.* Lawrence, KS: University Press of Kansas.

Holland, Margaret G. (1996) "What's Wrong with Telling the Truth? An Analysis of Gossip." *American Philosophical Quarterly* 33, no. 2, 197-209.

"Information Society Series Book: The Reputation Society," n.d. http://michaelzimmer.org/2012/01/24/information-society-series-book-the-reputation-society/, accessed 01 May 2012.

Ingram, Mathew. (2011) "Why Facebook's Frictionless Sharing Is the Future." *BusinessWeek*, October 3, http://www.businessweek.com/technology/why-facebooks-frictionless-sharing-is-the-future-10032011.html , accessed 10 April 2012.

Mill, J. S. (1869/1991). Of the Liberty of Thought and Discussion. In J. S. Mill, *Utilitarianism and Other Essays (ed J. Gray).* New York: Oxford University Press.

"Rumor and Gossip Research", n.d. http://www.apa.org/science/about/psa/2005/04/gossip.aspx , accessed 29 March 2012.

Solove, Daniel J. (2008) *The Future of Reputation: Gossip, Rumor, and Privacy on the Internet.* New Haven, CT: Yale University Press.

Sommerfeld, Ralf D., Hans-Jürgen Krambeck, Dirk Semmann, and Manfred Milinski. (2007) "Gossip as an Alternative for Direct Observation in Games of Indirect Reciprocity." *Proceedings of the National Academy of Sciences* 104, no. 44, 17435-17440.

Sulzberger, A. G. (2011) "Small-Town Gossip Moves to the Web, Anonymous and Vicious." *The New York Times*, September 19, sec. U.S. http://www.nytimes.com/2011/09/20/us/small-town-gossip-moves-to-the-web-anonymous-and-vicious.html , accessed 24 March 2012.

Thomas, Laurence. (1994) "The Logic of Gossip." In Goodman and Ben-Ze'ev, 47-55.

Vallor, Shannon. (2011) "Flourishing on Facebook: Virtue Friendship & New Social Media." *Ethics and Information Technology*, 1-15.

———. "Social Networking Technology and the Virtues." (2010) *Ethics and Information Technology* 12, no. 2, 157-170.

Westacott, Emrys. (2010) "The Ethics of Gossiping." *International Journal of Applied Philosophy* 14, no. 1, 65-90.

*III*

# Creating a Professional Truth

*Chapter Six*

# I Don't Do the News

*If Something Important Happens, My Friends Will Tell*
*Me on Facebook*

## Lee Wilkins

People now swim in an ocean of mediated communication. Journalism, too, may be becoming more liquid, at least in terms of who produces it. These developments place the current professional conceptualization of truth, which emerged from the Enlightenment, under pressure. The Enlightenment defined truth in terms of the scientific method employing a reductionistic epistemology. However, philosophers and neuroscientists suggest that complex systems provide a better metaphor for understanding the physical and mental world than Newton's clock. A post-Enlightenment construction of truth would reconnect emotion and reason and would promote an open ethics to develop standards of truth. Both of these elements, emotion connected to reason and an open source ethics, characterize a journalism of earned information. Facebook, as well as the *New York Times*, can be a repository of earned information. This conceptualization, in turn, reaffirms some and poses additional questions about journalism's link to truthtelling.

### HERACLITUS' TOES

Contemporary thinkers have nothing on Heraclitus. The Greek scholar, renowned through intellectual history for capturing the impact of change on human life, is often quoted as saying: "You can never step in the same river, for the water is always flowing on to you." People change, the river changes, change is the constant—not just in physics but in life. Or, as Bob Dylan rephrased it, "He who is not busy being born is busy dying."

In response to such insights, it is not surprising that the concept of truth, which has changed over the millennia (e.g. Plato, Augustine (1998), Kant as outlined in Underwood, 2003) but which has been relatively stable in human intellectual history since the Enlightenment, is under significant intellectual pressure. Professions, such as journalism, that draw their intellectual foundation from the Enlightenment find themselves under similar pressures. Much of the scholarship that attempts to encapsulate these pressures borrows the Heraclitus' metaphor: water, or more generically, liquid. Liquid communication platforms, and liquid journalism, provide a good starting place to understand an evolving definition of truth and how it might be expressed in the news and in social media.

Stephen G. Jones characterizes the contemporary media environment and human response to it as "swimming in an ocean," (Jones, personal communication). People move almost effortlessly—they swim—from television, to radio, to their computers, to legacy media, to social networks, to the telephone, to face-to-face conversation. The lines that have traditionally been drawn between devices and purposes melt under the efforts of an active audience that seeks information, entertainment, connection and citizenship (Blumer & Katz, 1974; Bugeja 2005) through a variety of platforms that are employed essentially for the same core purposes—some of them quite conscious (citizenship) and some of them much more instinctual (human connection). At their most fundamental level, the purposes of information, connection and citizenship also carry normative overtones. At their most robust, they make ethical claims. Jones's theoretical insight is significant: he suggests that human beings turn technology to their own purposes although the technology itself can influence how that turn is made. "We continue to face a predicament: How do we attend to the social, economic and political connections impinging on us, the connections we at once desire (e-mail, telephone, fax, democratic participation, business, etc.,) and that nurture our character as public beings and also despise (for they take up more and more of our time and energy and fragment privacy and self among a variety of publics)? Again, control is sought after, but it is not sought for the purposes of power but for the purposes of its inverse, restraint" (Jones 1998, p. 7). Thus, the communication ocean that contemporary humans swim in is not value neutral. In order to swim in that ocean, people must develop some conceptualization of reality and connection to help them achieve various purposes. Randomness in this environment is not merely counterproductive, it is almost nihilistic. It is not that there is "no" truth in the ocean, it is rather that how humans arrive at truth is emerging. It owes much to the past—the Enlightenment—but it is distinctive from it. Truth remains a fundamental ethical concept, even in this changing environment.

Similarly, some of the most recent scholarship on the role of journalism and of journalists relies on the water metaphor. Deuze, building on the scholarship of modernity, has introduced the phrase "liquid journalism" into the academic discussion. He notes:

> In journalism a similar trend is emerging, where traditional role perceptions of journalism influenced by its occupational ideology—providing a general audience with information of general interest in a balanced, objective and ethical way—do not seem to fit all that well with the lived realities of reporters and editors, nor with the communities they are supposed to serve. In the context of a precarious and, according to the International Federation of Journalists, increasingly "atypical" professional work life, ongoing efforts by corporations to merge and possibly converge news operations, and an emerging digital media culture where the consumer is also a producer of public information, the identity of the journalist must be seen as "liquid" (Bauman, 2000). Such a liquid journalism truly works in the service of the networked society, deeply respects the rights and privileges of each and every consumer-citizen to be a maker and user of his own news, and enthusiastically embraces its role as, to paraphrase James Carey, an "amplifier of the conversation society has with itself" (p. 848).

Deuze says that journalism as a profession is failing to come to grips with the volatile flux that the intersection of devices and human purposes represents. Furthermore, that professional change is taking place in a world that, at the individual and institutional level, has few touchstones. Liquid journalism, in Deuze's view, will push information at consumer/citizens (his word choice, not mine), in a media ecology that is uncertain and complex. While he says that he does not attempt to "retheorize" journalism in this new, liquid environment, Deuze does emphasize that it is the liquid context that is important. But, this new—or ancient—point of origin has ethical implications, predominant among them implications about the nature of truth. In a liquid environment, from a liquid professional role, how does one discover truth and how important is that discovery to the profession, the state and the culture? This chapter attempts to knit this idea of a liquid professional role and environment into an expanded conceptualization of truthful journalistic storytelling: earned information. Part of that truth is the incorporation of emotion into what has previously been characterized as objective reporting and editing. This inclusion of emotion, in addition to more traditional journalistic practice, results in a journalism of earned information: a kind of information that individual citizens are less likely to come by through even diligent searching for "facts" on their own. Earned information represents a non-reductionist standard of truth. Finally, the chapter will address the role of social media in uncovering and then sharing earned information.

## THE ENLIGHTENMENT AND THE MIND-ENHANCED BRAIN

The Enlightenment's conceptualization of truth cannot be adequately reviewed in anything shorter than a very long book. For purposes of this paper, the philosophical distinctions between the correspondence theory of truth, the co-relational theory of truth and the coherence theory of truth, plus the scientific-method approach to finding truth, will be largely ignored. All of them find their epistemological foundation in the Enlightenment, and all of them are employed daily by journalists (for a good, professionally oriented review see Bugeja, 2008). They fund a core understanding that has taken more than 400 years to develop (Ward, 2004) and which continues to dominate current professional practice.

When professional journalists think about truth, allowing for individual variations, the following conceptualization emerges:

- Truth has an empirical basis;
- Truth is knowable by individuals and outside of the realm of religion;
- Truth can be ascertained through observation and measurement;
- No one person may know the entire truth, but a combination of in-person observations, discussion with those involved, and a review of empirical data will generate truth;
- Truth is seldom singular; it may take it a while to emerge;
- Truth has a strong connection to evidence and a willingness to make evidence public;
- Truth is predominantly logical; arriving at truth can be a process;
- Truth is knowable incrementally. Incremental acquisition of truth, as it is connected to knowledge, is both a process and an end;
- Truth is stable across individual perceptions and experiences which is not to say that it is *identical* to different individuals but that it is coherent and shared among individuals;
- Truth is preserved in written form. Writing, in the professional context, may and often does include visual images and audio content;
- Truth motivates people to act, particularly in the realm of citizenship;
- Truth is a core, perhaps *the* core, professional value (Patterson & Wilkins, 2011; Christians et al, 2008; Borden 2007).

Were a philosopher to examine this outline of journalistic truth, there would be much to debate. But, as a professional rule of thumb, it has worked imperfectly for more than 100 years. And, there is little reason to believe that a more philosophically rigorous approach would work out any better in professional application. Journalists do not have to be in the profession long to understand Sissela Bok's reminder:

Telling the "truth" therefore is not solely a matter of moral character; it is also a matter of correct appreciation of real situations and of serious reflection upon them...Telling the truth, therefore, is something which must be learnt. This will sound very shocking to anyone who thinks that it must all depend on moral character and that if this is blameless the rest is child's play. But the simple fact is that the ethics cannot be detached from reality, and consequently continual progress in learning to appreciate reality is a necessary ingredient in ethical action (Bok 1978, p. 302-303).

## THE WHOLE IS GREATER THAN THE SUM OF ITS PARTS

By peeling back the layers of the Enlightenment epistemological onion, it becomes possible to understand the impact of the "liquid" system on the Enlightenment construct. Epistemologically, the Enlightenment approach has favored a kind of division. At the most gross level (and among the most criticized) is the severing of logic from emotion. Many trace this demarcation to Descartes (1641-1642/1978). At the level of the scientific method, there is the approach of dividing large problems into their component parts, studying the parts, and then reassembling a "coherent" whole. This is the standard academic approach in the sciences, social sciences and philosophy, and it is mimicked by the concept of "the daily" news. The result is what philosophers call a reductionist approach to knowledge: that by understanding component parts, it is possible to understand the whole. Logic dominates this understanding, and knowing is the province of the individual, not of any collection of individuals or of a community.

Nancey Murphy notes there are multiple sorts of reductionism: methodological, epistemological, causal and ontological (Murphy & Brown, 2007, p. 47). Journalists accept that no single story may convey *all* the truth, but that an accumulation of stories over months and years will at least get individual readers/viewers/listeners closer to it. If I want to understand how Columbia, Missouri, approaches urban development, attending a single city council meeting will not provide me with much information. But, reading news accounts for a year, as they happen, will get me much closer to that understanding, to a preliminary grasp of a "truth". It may even provide me with opportunities to participate. I have used a reductionist method—daily news—to explore the component parts of the politics of urban development through individual news stories and a single political entity—epistemological reductionism—to understand how the city government as an institution will respond to development issues—causal reductionism.

It would be foolish to discard such an accumulation of intellectual wealth. But, these epistemological assumptions also rule out other ways of knowing and hence understanding or discovering truth. Chief among them is downward causation, or what is also referred to as a non-reductive world view.

Phrased colloquially, it means the whole is greater than the sum of its parts. As biologists understand it, downward causation means that the initial conditions in which complex systems find themselves are at least as important to understanding those systems as the investigation of the processes that transpire within complex systems. Downward causation "recognizes that complex wholes can be more than aggregates. It employs the concepts of boundary conditions, structures, information, feedback...." (Murphy & Brown, 2007, p. 67).

## The Interaction of Social Media and the Mind-Enhanced Brain

Social media in all their permutations constitute such a complex, world-wide system. Social media—again recall the "liquid metaphor"—are a component part of a complex system that may include everything from interpersonal communication (talking to friends) to mass mediated information (the front page of the *New York Times* as it reports the latest crackdown on social media discussion of political dissidents in China). Social media constitute a liquid that is, at once, an initial condition that must be considered, a potential information gathering opportunity, and a potential information dissemination platform. And, social media interact with another complex system—what neuroscientists refer to as the mind-enhanced brain.

Pamela Shoemaker in the last decade of the twentieth century suggested that the human mind was hardwired for news (1996). She traced these developments equally to evolutionary and cultural roots: people need news to survive in the environment and they need news to make sense of the human-created culture that constitutes much of that environment in both the twentieth and the twenty-first centuries. Shoemaker made her argument without much reference to neuroscience, but in the ensuing years, findings in that field have accumulated to the point where any serious discussion of human ethical response to external conditions must take into account what neuroscience has learned about what Darwin first characterized as "the moral organ." Again, reviewing all of this work, some of it still emerging and some of it quite controversial, is beyond the scope of this paper. But, for the present purposes, the following understandings appear consistent across individual scholars and specific disciplines.

- The capacity for moral thinking, just like the capacity for language, appears to be hardwired in the human brain (Hauser 2006);
- The human brain is a dynamic, organic system. What this means is that the organic mind is plastic—it can and does grow and change depending on initial conditions and in response to subsequent ones. Moral thinking develops, just as the capacity for language develops: (Rest et al 1999; Erikson, Piaget, Kohlberg, 1981, 1984; Gilligan, 1982);

- Moral thinking—and moral action—involve the emotions as well as "rational" thought (Gazzaniga 2005, 2011; Hauser 2006; Hume, 1739; Hoffman, 2001);
- Although early work suggested that rational thought was processed separately in the human brain from emotion, new research suggests that both elements are processed simultaneously and in the same hemispheres of the brain. In other words, moral thinking engages much of the complex organic system that is the human brain, summoning both logic and emotion.

Gazzaniga summarizes it this way: "We should look for a universal ethics comprising not hard-and-fast truths, but for the universal ethics that arises from being human, which is clearly contextual, emotion influenced and designed to increase our survival (Gazzaniga, 2005, p. 177). In his later work, Gazzaniga specifically links moral thinking to understanding the emotions of others and to the profoundly social nature of human beings (2011).

Moral thinking, under the insights of neuroscience, is a complex system. Professional moral thinking, then, needs to consider initial conditions—the liquid channels of communication and the potential of a more liquid professional role—as they interact with the complex system that is the mind-enhanced brain and human culture. In doing so, it becomes impossible to ignore that people are social beings and one important element of the social nature of the species is an ability to incorporate emotion into moral decision making. These insights have important implications for the discovery and the transmission of truth in a professional context that serves civic function: journalism. In addition, because systems constitute the core of the intellectual problem, downward logic—an epistemology that considers the whole before subdividing it into various parts—seems appropriate.

Thus, instead of abandoning the hard-won insights of the Enlightenment, particularly when it comes to understanding the concept of truth, post-Enlightenment thinking would suggest building on those concepts from the view of the system and then considering how those theoretical insights can be applied in the "parts" that comprise the system but do not explain it in its entirety. Under even the best of circumstances, telling the truth is a complicated, demanding process for professionals. It requires both thinking and acting, and the necessity of doing both in the professional realm is one key to understanding how the concept itself is changing.

# RECONCEPTUALIZING TRUTH: JOURNALISM'S ROLE IN A SOCIAL AND CULTURAL SYSTEM

Dewey (1954; Welchman 1995) suggested that journalism should have a "progressive" role in American culture. By progressive, Dewey did not mean the acquisition of technology—his notion was comprised of almost equal parts smart government and the more equal distribution of collective goods throughout American society. In other words, journalism was to provide information that would spark action: it had a social, collective purpose. This notion of journalism linked to political actions of various sorts is pervasive in media ethics scholarship (see, for example, Christians, Glasser, McQuail, Nordenstreng & White, 2009) and certainly serves as a lynchpin for the role that truthful information is required to play in a democratic political system. However, neuroscience consistently finds that moral action—indeed in many instances moral thinking—cannot be separate from the emotions. To promote action, journalism cannot be separated from the emotions in the way that objectivity, which takes its cue from an Enlightenment conceptualization of truth, traditionally has been defined. Rorty thought that narrative had a role in connecting fact and emotion to a larger, conceptual truth. The stories that journalists tell can have a similar function. James Ettema (2009), quotes Rorty to this purpose: "narrative . . . facilitates . . . imaginative identification with the details of others lives and thereby promotes a loathing for cruelty, a sense of the contingency of selfhood and of history, and beyond that, a sense of human solidarity" (Ettema, 2009, p. 123). Narrative—storytelling with a public purpose which is the role of journalism—incorporates emotion as well as fact, not only in story construction but also in reaction to those stories.

There are multiple examples of such journalistic efforts, but the point is that based on the understandings of neuroscience and viewed from the perspective of the system, truth and emotion need to be reunited in a single concept that is not reducible to emotion on one side and logic on the other. This inability to reduce also means that emotion remains informed by logic just as logic remains informed by emotion. Both are connected to the bedrock of ethical thought that is hardwired in the mind-enhanced brain. The result, here, looks much more like analysis than it does a mere reporting of individual and disconnected facts.

Journalists already have a vocabulary for one version of this approach: investigative reporters call it the system story—journalism that combines both analysis and compelling narrative. As former journalist Jack Fuller, who has also called for journalists to be "less afraid" of emotion says, "Arguments, too, are flat or round. The flat ones grind on in a totally predictable way. The flat liberal or conservative, the flat fundamentalist or atheist not only sees everything through an ideological lens, all he sees is the lens. No stray light comes through. No challenge to the orthodoxy. Round arguments, on the other hand, respond to the complexity of event. They recognize the limitations of their own assumptions. They may veer in unexpected directions, not in pursuit of novelty, but in response to data that challenges the well-trod path of their general approach" (Fuller 2010, p. 151). Investigative reporting demands action, not just contemplation. Emotion, for both the journalist and the audience members, is involved (Ettema & Glasser, 1998).

## CONNECTING EMOTION AND LOGIC TO TRUTH

Connecting emotion with fact to derive a larger and more holistic truth that is often found in narrative also opens up journalistic forms. First-person, point-of-view journalism—the approach of many audio and visual documentaries—deliberately captures the connection between emotion and facts while simultaneously revealing the journalists' connection to each. Such work speaks to the senses, and to the sense of intimacy that oral communication creates. When emotion and logic are connected within a larger concept—in this case truth—then a profession that has prided itself on a certain sort of intellectual detachment becomes able to reconnect to its professional role and standards of excellence in new, and in this instance converged, ways. The ethical concept remains the same, but it is expanded beyond its Enlightenment articulation. (For examples of this work, see documentary films such as Born into Brothels, Enemies of the People and The Devil Rides on Horseback or audio documentaries such as Habeus Schmaebeus or Ghetto Life.) The professional challenge is to connect fact to emotion and to construct a narrative that takes both into account. Merely evoking individual rage or disgust is not the goal of such journalism, although sometimes this is the result. But, the larger goal is a holistic truth—one that is centered in community as much as it is in the individual and one that helps communities to articulate civic obligations and potentials. This is the sort of ethical professional standard that requires a "firm handshake with the emotions."

In some instances, this expansion includes non-traditional journalists who "do" non-traditional journalism: in this case holding the institution of journalism itself to account. Part of what makes Jon Stewart's work *feel* like journalism is the fact it performs a very journalistic function—holding a democratic society's institutions to account—specifically the institution of journalism itself (Painter & Hodges, 2012). This is the systems story, applying the downward logic of an understanding of the journalistic role, and examining the parts in light of this greater whole. This is not to suggest that everything that Stewart does meets these criteria; it is to say that it is a consistent, stable part of *The Daily Show* that audiences themselves appear to have connected with on both a cognitive and emotional way. Stewart provides his viewers with a truth *about how the media themselves work* and does so using a post-Enlightenment view of truth, one that includes facts connected to emotion and informed by it.

This view of the system also means that ethical standards will develop in a complex, interactive way involving more than just traditional, legacy journalists (Ward & Wasserman, 2012). As Borden (2007), Bugeja (2005, 2008) and Friend & Singer (2007) among others note, the pressures of the web have forced traditional journalists to confront—and then expand—their traditional ways of knowing. Borden says, "Intellectual practices—such as science, journalism and teaching—cooperatively determine what counts as a particular kind of knowledge, what is worthy of investigation, what is worthy of dissemination, and in what form. Each, in its own sphere is engaged in seeking and sharing an authoritative account of the 'truth'. It is this knowledge quest, how it is conducted and how it is internally and externally validated that constitute the essence of science, on the one hand, on journalism on the other." Borden and others note that science is produced in a "complex network of interdependence" (Borden, 2007, p. 61). In other words, what is discovered in one place is capable of correction in another—a liquid network of knowledge.

Ward and Wasserman suggest that this interactive system will soon—if it does not already—apply not just to information collection but to the development of ethical standards. The work of legacy journalists is already corrected, supported and expanded by the blogosphere. Crowd sourcing, on some sort of stories, is now standard journalistic process. Whether journalists will even willingly open their ethical standards to review and correction in this same way is an important question, but the emerging understanding of the help that bloggers, user generated content, etc., can contribute to more accurate, if not better, journalism seems no longer in much doubt. Accuracy and completeness are not synonymous with truth, but they are among its component elements. The web certainly makes this sort of conversation more possible than it was even a decade ago; the furor over the changing privacy rules on Facebook provides at least one anecdote to suggest that the audience is willing to become involved, and, in fact, will not tolerate a lack of involvement. In fits and starts, the same thing appears to be happening about truth.

## THE NEWS AND FACEBOOK

Read the title of this paper to a journalist or an academic who teaches journalism and one of two things is likely to occur: a guffaw or a groan. The groan is more readily understandable, for journalists know how much work it is to gather the news, accept that the effort is best left in the hands of professionals, and realize, simultaneously, that people would rather spend their time catching up with friends on Facebook than—let's face it—reading the *New York Times*. Take, for example, this response by an English professor to a question in the "Daily Read" column of the *Chronicle of Higher Education*:

> This might strike you as bizarre, but I've discovered over the past couple of years that Facebook often makes for a better reading experience of the news than anything else. Your friends have already curated for you news from all over the world, and also provided links to interesting magazine articles. In many cases, you get this news accompanied by comments from other friends that you like.
>
> Nevertheless, I still subscribe to the Times, which I get at my doorstep daily, and magazines like *The New Yorker, London Review of Books, Harper's,* and *The New York Review of Books*. However, my reading of these is quite uneven, and I sometimes come to them after I've encountered their virtual avatars. (quoted in Kumar 2010).

The guffaw seems directed simultaneously at message and messenger. There is an incredible amount of junk on Facebook, and more is appearing every day. As the film *The Social Network* makes clear, Facebook was originally intended to help people find partners—however briefly—and to form connections and barriers between in-groups and out-groups, individually defined. But, much of that effort was devoted to non-civic communication: I'm eating a sandwich. Journalists are unimpressed with the solipsism involved and the often trivial nature of what was conveyed. Now, about 800 million entities, from people, to products, to NGOs, to governments, to churches, to schools, to corporations, to political candidates, to news organizations, have a Facebook page. In a demonstrable sense, Facebook now is as much a mall and a place for front-stage communication (Meyrowitz, 1986) as it is a place for the more intimate, serendipitous communication that enabled people to connect with each other.

Journalists also understand at a visceral level what Facebook and the internet more generally have meant to the profession. Now, everyone can and does collect facts—readers/listeners/viewers no longer need a journalistic intermediary to do that. Audience members can do it for free—or at least at the cost of their time and effort as opposed to coin. Or, as one of my former students told me the day after his paper, the *Rocky Mountain News*, folded, "There was this woman—a neighbor—who told me, 'Well, I'm sorry the paper is closing, but I'll still read you on line.'" Many in the public disconnected the fact that legacy journalists were the ones producing on-line content and that, without them, that contribution to an ocean of information would evaporate. Someone—human or algorithm—has to do the work. And, even the algorithm has to search for something that a human being has produced.

There may also be some envy. Who among us has the sort of friends who have the time to post on our Facebook walls the equivalent of Negroponte's (1996) *The Daily Me*. It is friends serving as a highly personal aggregator, for human beings who, in this instance, are demonstrably lazy and too prone to group think. But, just like the English professor quoted in the Chronicle, many get at least some, or all, news from Facebook friends. So, if everybody can collect information, and has a really willing circle of friends, why (or do) democracies need the profession of journalism?

Borden (2007) ties that need to the act of reporting. Journalism has always been about getting information to people that it would be difficult or sometimes impossible for them to collect themselves. The distinguishing activity of journalism as practice, Borden writes, "is reporting. Like all practices, journalism relies for excellence on a set of skills, a vocational aspect, and certain institutional resources. Journalism's immediate goal is to create the public sphere; journalists produce and disseminate this knowledge in the form of 'news.' News is defined in terms of a communitarian account of participatory citizenship . . . " (p. 138). What Borden does not say—because she is writing for journalists—is that reporting is more than just fact collecting from whatever computer screen an individual happens to be connected to. Reporting is about talking to others, it is about collecting facts over time which produces, among other things, the beginning of a context, it is about putting facts together with opinion in such a way as they inform one other. More important, it is also about collecting, facts, opinion, and learning about topics that are relatively uninteresting to the individual journalists. It is about talking to and trying to think like others who are very unlike individual journalists. It is as much about a systematic method of inquiry as it is a passion-fueled drive for the truth about only closely circumscribed issues. It is literally professional practice. In this sense, the practice of reporting is about as far removed from talking exclusively to Facebook friends as a professional activity is likely to become.

Borden's insight in the internet age translates to earned information as the defining quality of news. Earned information is much closer to the systems story than to daily events. Its coin of the realm is not fact collection but analysis and context. Earned information, then, also deliberately summons emotion to the truth behind the facts. Earned information remains information that it would be difficult for individuals to collect, not because they could not assemble the facts from the internet but because assembling the facts (from non-digitized sources as well) does not capture the whole picture. So, for earned information to inch toward truth, it must also incorporate the top-down logic of systems and initial conditions rather than events. It also, to a greater or lesser degree, must acknowledge the global as well as the local— because that is the ocean of the internet. This is the more stringently cognitive quality of earned information: it is the news of analysis and perspective.

Merely shipping news content from one website to another—in this case a Facebook page—does not meet the demands of earned information. But, shipping news from one site to a Facebook page—with comments or an implied endorsement—might begin to do that.

## Providing Context to Earned Information

Earned information is probably best "packaged" in a narrative form. Narrative provides a context, and to that it sometimes adds the quality of foregrounding the underlying surveillance, citizenship and connection issues that form the heart of most "stories" that people appear to seek out. Point-of-view reporting and audio and video documentaries—journalistic forms that have become prominent in the last decade—fulfill this element of earned information. First-person and point-of-view reporting also have a quality of transparency: audience members can "see" where the reporter is coming from. They provide a narrative and a context in which to understand it. So does some entertainment—or what scholars have traditionally labeled entertainment—programming. The "truthiness" of *The Colbert Report*, for scholars and audience members, is understood within a parody narrative. Some of Stewart's *The Daily Show* segments are understood within a context of irony. Both provide lessons in media literacy; they point out where individual media stories (the parts) miss the whole of truth and, by implication, they provide that truth through critique. This is not to say that more traditional journalistic narrative does not have a place in the narrative effort. First-person and point-of-view reporting provide eloquent examples. But, the second sort of narrative reporting has a long and distinguished history, dating back at least to the cultural commentary of Johnson or the satiric political analysis of Jonathan Swift.

To promote action of any sort—whether it is civic action or a more immediate surveillance or connection functions that may not be overtly political—earned information must deal with emotion. Those who produce such information must accept that emotional content is inextricably part of what makes such information actionable to individuals. In fact, they should make an effort to thoughtfully incorporate emotion into information. The refusal to separate emotion from cognition is particularly crucial when potential action incorporates an ethical choice of the sort Ettema (2009) describes. For information to be earned, it can no longer afford to avoid the emotional impact sets of facts within a context do have. The irreducible truth, what Christians (2010) describes as one of three protonorms underlying all ethical communication, accepts emotion as part of the concept because it is emotion that will promote action. It is the sort of truth that Gandhi described: it is motivating at the individual and community level. For reporting to have the sort of civic impact, it must provide people with a reason to act. And, the system of the mind-enhanced brain harnesses emotion for that purpose. This is a systemic, non-reductionistic window into what will genuinely constitute news in the internet environment. Earned information, then, is telling system stories with a larger social and political purpose, connecting the system to individuals and calling individuals and groups to action through the emotion that narrative arouses. It is what journalists mean when they call themselves story tellers.

Social media, of course, have a role in this process. They can be a repository for ideas about potential stories (http://stateofthemedia.org/2012/mobile-devices-and-news-consumption-some-good-signs-for-journalism/what-facebook-and-twitter-mean-for-news/) and social media already serve as a source repository—a way of connecting journalists to sources (expert and naïve) that they would unable to tap in any other way. But, using social media as the exclusive curator of news for individuals can be problematic—something individuals appear already to have realized. More and more, people access social media on their mobile devices—a use of technology that should unsurprising for a special as social and human beings. But, if the latest studies are accurate, when individuals receive information on their mobile devices and including through the Facebook pages, they turn frequently to traditional journalistic sites to follow up. And, only about 10% of Facebook users say that the allow their Facebook friends to be the curators of news. In other words, learning about something on Facebook becomes a portal to seeking the sort of earned information that professionals can and do provide—with the information that the information environment itself has become so liquid that it must now be considered an "initial condition" in which journalism itself plays out.

## The Liquification of Journalism

Journalists themselves are going to have to be willing to relinquish their complete control over the standards of what constitutes "earned information." In this sense, information has to be earned by the larger community, not just the professionals involved. This is the sort of open-source ethics that Ward and Wasserman suggest, and for journalists it can be extraordinarily problematic and discouraging. It is one of the profoundly unintended consequences of the "liquification" of both the message and the messenger; people who lack professional training and whose intellectual credentials are atypical are now demanding to be treated as the ethical equals of professionals who have spent lifetimes wrestling with the difficult problem of discovering and conveying truth in the form of news to a broad audience. To have this effort usurped by "amateurs" is professionally debilitating. But, it is part of the systemic—liquid—reality in which journalists now find themselves. The truth of the message, thus, is going to become far more a process of negotiation among stakeholders than the Enlightenment definition has ever been.

Getting news from my Facebook friends may be the beginning of that process of negotiating about the standards of truthful communication, and hence journalism. But, the process itself is crude, and it is far from clear at this point how it might be subject to correction, interpretation or—most importantly—plural points of view.

There are, of course, problems with this concept of earned information. Because it is in some significant ways set in opposition to the Enlightenment professional praxis, earned information misses the mark of truth by about the same margin as the definition professionals are currently working with, just in different ways. There are additional, and significant questions, among them whether such an approach can be monetized in a viral environment. But, the most significant among them falls back on the nature of Facebook itself lodged as it is within the system of the internet:

- Does the internet itself, and the way the human mind accesses and understands internet content, change the concept of narrative itself? That is one of the assertions Nicholas Carr (2010), based on emerging but by no means definitive work that combines traditional cognition research with neuroscience, has made;
- What is it that might motivate me to move beyond a familiar and emotionally satisfying narrative to an unfamiliar context that might promote a different sort of action? And, if the context with which I am most familiar and comfortable, as are my friends, is one that eschews political action for the comforts of the moment, what must happen for me to engage in the political community of which I am an inextricable part?

These are serious questions. But, they are not so different from the ones the Enlightenment conceptualization of the truth poses. Getting news on the internet in the form of unthinking reinforcement from a too-small circle of friends is the same problem that interpersonal communication has faced—sans technology—for hundreds, if not thousands, of years. Poor answers have led to demagoguery and tyranny of the worst sort. Demagogues and tyrants have always asserted that "they" have the truth, and most often the media of the day have supported them. Enlightenment understandings of truth made such domination by no means impossible, but much, much more difficult. The question remains whether the internet will be one tool that will allow humanity to construct a social system that will do more to support individual ethical action while retarding the unethical. Getting your news from Facebook may seem laughable, but those liquid initial conditions may exert profound influences on professionals and audiences alike. Earned information as a systemic, non-reductionist standard for journalistic truth may not be such a bad place to start.

# REFERENCES

Augustine, St. Bishop of Hippo. (1998). *The City of God against the pagans*. Ed. and translated by R. W. Dyson, Cambridge: Cambridge University Press.

Bauman, Z. (2000). *Liquid modernity*. Cambridge: Polity Press.

Blumer, J. G., & Katz, E. 1974. *The uses of mass communication: Current perspectives on gratifications research*. Sage: Beverly Hills.

Bok, S. (1978). *Lying: Moral choice in public and private life*. New York: Random House.

Borden, Sandra L. (2007). *Journalism as practice: MacIntyre, virtue ethics and the press*. Burlington, VT: Ashgate.

Bugeja, M. (2005). *Inter-personal divide*. Oxford: Oxford University Press.

Bugeja, M. (2008). *Living ethics: Across media platforms*. Oxford: Oxford University Press.

Carr, N. (2010). *The Shallows: What the internet is doing to our brains*. New York: W. W. Norton & Co.

Christians, C.G. (2010). Response: Theories of morality in three dimensions, in *Ethics and Evil in the Public Sphere*, eds. Robert Fortner and Mark Fackler, Cresskill, N. J.: Hampton Press, Inc., pp. 335-346.

Christians, C.G.; Glasser, Theodore, L.; McQuail, D.; Nordenstreg, K., & White, R. A. (2009). *Normative theories of the media: Journalism in democratic societies*. Urbana: University of Illinois Press.

Christians, C.G; Fackler, M.; Richarson, K. R.; Kreshel, P. J., and Woods, R. H. (2008). *Media Ethics: Cases and Moral Reasoning* (8th Edition). New York: Allyn and Bacon.

Descartes, R. (1978). *Meditations concerning first philosophy*. New York: Dutton. (Original work published 1641-1642).

Deuze, M. (2008). The changing context of news work: Liquid journalism and monitorial citizenship. International Journal of Communication 2: 848-865.

Dewey, J. (1954). *The public and its problems*. Chicago: The Swallow Press.

Erikson, E. H. (1964). *Childhood and society*. New York: Norton.

Ettema, J. (2009). The moment of truthiness: The right time to consider the meaning of truthfulness, in Editor Barbie Zelizer, *The Changing faces of journalism: Tabloidization, technology and truthiness*, London: Routledge, pp114-126.

Ettema, J.S., & Glasser, T. L. (1998). *Custodians of conscience: Investigative journalism and public virtue*. New York: Columbia University Press.

Friend, C., & Singer, J. (2007). *On-line media ethics: Traditions and transitions*. New York: M. E. Sharpe.

Fuller, Jack. (2010). *What is happening to news: The information explosion and the crisis in journalism*. Chicago: University of Chicago Press.

Gazzaniga, M. S. (2005). *The ethical brain: The science of our moral dilemmas*. New York: Dana Press.

Gazzaniga, M. S. (2011). *Who's in charge: Free will and the science of the brain*. New York: HarperCollins.

Gilligan, Carol. (1982). *In a different voice: Psychological theory and women's development*. Cambridge, MA.: Harvard University Press.

Hauser, Marc D. (2006). *Moral minds: How nature designed our universal sense of right and wrong*. New York: HarperCollins.

Hoffman, M. (2001). *Empathy and moral development: Implications for care and justice*. Cambridge: Cambridge University Press.

Hume, David. (1739/1977). *A treatise of human nature*. Oxford: Oxford University Press.

Jones, S. G. (2006, April). Personal communication. Grand Rapids, Michigan.

Jones, S. G., ed. (1998). *Cybersociety 2.0: Revisiting computer mediated communication and community*. Thousand Oaks, CA: Sage.

Kohlberg, L. (1981). *Essays on moral development, Vol. 1: The philosophy of moral development*. New York: Harper & Row.

Kohlberg, L. (1984). *The psychology of moral development: The nature and validity of moral stages*. San Francisco: Harper & Row.

Kumar, A. (2010). My Daily Read. Chronicle of Higher Education, September 17, p. B2.

Meyrowitz, J. (1986). *No sense of place: The impact of electronic media on social behavior.* Oxford: Oxford University Press.

Mitchell, A.; Rosenstiel, T., & Christian, L. (2012). http://stateofthemedia.org/2012/mobile-devices-and-news-consumption-some-good-signs-for-journalism/what-facebook-and-twitter-mean-for-news/

Murphy N., & Brown, W. S. (2007). *Did my neurons make me do it?* Oxford: Oxford University Press.

Negroponte, N. (1996). *Being digital.* New York: Vintage.

Painter, C., & Hodges, L. (2012). Mocking the news: How *The Daily Show with Jon Stewart* holds traditional broadcast news accountable, in *Media Accountability: Who will watch the Watchdog in the Twitter Age?* Ed. William A. Babcock. New York: Taylor & Francis, pp. 1-18.

Patterson, P., & Wilkins, L. (2011). *Media ethics: Issues and cases.* New York: Mc-Graw Hill.

Piaget, J. (1965 [1932]). *The moral judgment of the child.* New York: The Free Press.

Plato. *The Republic.*

Rest, J.R., Narvaez, D., Bebeau, M.J. & Thoma, S.J. (1999). *Postconventional moral thinking: A neo-Kohlbergian approach.* Mahwah, NJ: Lawrence Erlbaum Associates.

Shoemaker, P. J. (1996). Hardwired for News: Using Biological and Cultural Evolution to Explain the Surveillance Function. Journal of Communication 46, 3; 32-47.

Underwood, L. J. (2003). *Kant's correspondence theory of truth.* New York: Peter Lang.

Ward, S. J. A. (2004). *The invention of journalism ethics.* Toronto: McGill University Press.

Ward, S. J. A. & Wasserman, H. (2012). Towards an open ethics: Implications of new media platforms for global ethics discourse, in *Media Accountability: Who will watch the Watchdog in the Twitter Age?* Ed. William A. Babcock. New York: Taylor & Francis, pp. 19-38.

Welchman, J. (1995). *Dewey's ethical thought.* Ithaca & London: Cornell University Press.

*Chapter Seven*

# "It's About Trust"

*Should Government Intervene to Compel Disclosure in Social Media?*

## Jane Kirtley

The explosion of the use of social media, including blogs, Facebook and Twitter, has challenged conventional ethical practices for the so-called "legacy" news media. On the one hand, journalists are encouraged by their managers to engage with their readers through a variety of platforms, especially the latest digital forms of interactive communication, where "edgy" postings can drive traffic to an institutional web site. On the other hand, these often unmediated communications are fraught with potential problems, both legal and ethical. Among the obvious legal concerns are the possibilities of publishing material that could be libelous or invade someone's privacy, or which violates another's copyright interests. Perhaps less obvious risks include inadvertently disclosing the identity of confidential sources, or breaching editorial "privacy" by revealing newsgathering strategies prematurely.

But social media use also offers the risk, or perhaps the opportunity, of breaking down the illusion of "objectivity." Long touted as the gold standard of journalism in the United States, the ideal of objectivity has been questioned increasingly by media critics of all political stripes, many of whom maintain that no journalist or news organization is truly unbiased. It would be better, they argue, for journalists to adopt a new transparency, express viewpoints, and reveal their affiliations and prejudices so that readers may judge for themselves the fairness and accuracy of the reporting (Empson, 2011; Poniewozik, 2010).

Nevertheless, many "mainstream" or "legacy" news organizations contin-ue to cleave to the objectivity standard, although they find it challenging to maintain that standard in the social media environment. In 2009, the *Wall Street Journal*, the Associated Press, the *Washington Post*, and National Public Radio, as well as trade associations like the Radio Television Digital News Association, among others, were some of the first to promulgate rules or guidelines governing journalists' use of social media. Some versions are free standing and specifically labeled as such; others are revisions of existing standards and practices. But in either case, they have been controversial, with one critic dismissing the new rules as nothing less than an attempt to "squelch the right to be spontaneous" (Sullivan, 2009).

Typical guidelines include some or all of the following:

- Journalists must identify themselves as journalists, and reveal their institu-tional affiliation
- Posting material about the news organization's internal operations is for-bidden
- Information obtained from social media sources must be independently confirmed
- Reporters should not editorialize about topics or people they cover
- Care must be taken when registering for social network sites, because profiles can reveal information that can be misinterpreted by viewers
- "Friending" or "liking" sources or news subjects (such as a politician or a political web site) can create the appearance of bias or conflicts of interest.

Although many of these provisions reflect ethical standards regarding jour-nalists avoiding affiliations or other conflicts of interest that were already in place—"[d]on't march in protests, don't contribute to a political campaign, don't stick a political placard on your front lawn"—others are specifically adapted to the realities of the new media environment (Podger, 2009). The Associated Press original "social media" guidelines, issued in June 2009, apply to all employees, not just journalists, because "[w]e cannot expect people outside the AP to know whether a posting on Facebook was made by someone who takes pictures, processes payroll checks or fixes satellite dishes. We all represent AP and we all must protect its reputation." The guidelines prohibit posting "material about the AP's internal operations . . . on employees' personal pages," and require those employees to monitor their Facebook pages to be sure that "material posted by others doesn't violate AP standards; any such material should be deleted" (Strupp, 2009).

## NEW GUIDELINES CRITICIZED BY MEMBERS OF PRESS

Shortly after they were announced, the guidelines were attacked by leaders of the News Media Guild, which represents more than one thousand AP employees in the United States, as an overreaching attempt to abridge the employees' free speech rights and to short-circuit the very conversations that the social media were intended to encourage (Strupp, 2009). Similarly, the Philadelphia Newspaper Guild blasted the social networking policy adopted by the *Philadelphia Inquirer* and *Daily News*, asserting that it was an attempt to unilaterally impose new terms and conditions of employment and illegally interfered with the Guild members' rights to express their personal views— especially about management (Strupp, 2010b).

The Guild's concerns were not without foundation. For example, Ed Padgett, a 38-year employee at the *Los Angeles Times*, was suspended after he wrote about production problems at the newspaper on the pressroom employees' blog (Roderick, 2010). An Associated Press reporter was reprimanded after he posted a comment to his Facebook profile criticizing management at McClatchy, a member of AP's newsgathering cooperative (Alexander, 2009).

But these disciplinary actions, associated with commentary on the business or management of the journalist's employer, are arguably distinguishable from commentary on the news that the reporter covers. Jeff Jarvis, inveterate blogger, media critic, and director of the interactive journalism program at the City University of New York, has argued that policies like the *Wall Street Journal's*, which require approval by an editor before reporters "friend" any confidential sources and prohibit publication of details of how a story was written or about interviews conducted, "miss[es] the chance to make their reporting collaborative. Of course, they should discuss how an article was made. Of course, they should talk about stories as they progress. Twitter, blogs, Facebook, etc., also provide the opportunity for reporters and editors to come out from behind the institutional voice of the paper—a voice that is less and less trusted—and to become human" (Gahran, 2009).

By contrast, many would agree with Lex Alexander, a former journalist turned public relations practitioner who writes Blog on the Run: Reloaded, who observed, "[P]osting online about your day job is really not a good idea. You just never know what kind of innocuous remark is going to set someone off," and "journalists, for better or worse . . . can't really post online about issues they cover in any way that could be construed as taking a position on the merits of someone's argument" (2009).

## ETHICAL EXPECTATIONS FOR BLOGGERS

But whatever the relative merits of the competing positions, it is clear that legacy news organizations are thinking hard and seriously about the ethical challenges raised by the use of social media. What is less certain is that amateur bloggers who are not steeped in these traditions and standards will follow them as well, or even recognize them as problematic if they do not.

For example, newsroom ethical codes generally devote several paragraphs, if not pages, to a discussion of how to deal with "freebies" of various kinds, often associated with reviews of products, services, and artistic performances and sporting events: tickets, travel, meals, books, or the like. Many news organizations have traditionally prohibited reporters from accepting anything at all, requiring that the items be returned or donated to charity. At the very least, full disclosure that goods or services were received free of charge would be mandated, under the theory that the reader or viewer can add this fact to her assessment of whether the report or review is fair and unbiased. Clearly, accepting payments or a commission from commercial or other entities in exchange for writing a favorable review would be out of the question.

The Ethics Code for News/Editorial Employees at the *Austin (Texas) American-Statesman* is illustrative. It includes a lengthy provision headed "Reviewing versus Selling," which with some shortening reads as follows:

> At times, staff members will be writing about products that are for sale. When these reviews are for the paper, they undergo the strong scrutiny of our editing process and appear in a context that makes it clear they are news. When these reviews are unedited, as they are for blogs, Twitter and other social media, writers should be deliberative about whether their words can be misconstrued as advertising a product or a store. There is a particular danger in presenting information without a lot of context under the space constraints of something like Twitter. A Tweet that says "DVDs are 20 percent off at Target" from a *Statesman*-affiliated account is more likely to be seen as an advertisement than a news item, so as a rule we should avoid it. Such Tweets could present a conflict of mission between editorial and advertising departments and suggest bias or erode credibility of our staff. Some beat writers who are considered consumer experts in their area (personal technology, food, gardening, etc.) may at times want to let their followers know about deals that, because they are so extraordinary, constitute news (ex: "Wii prices have dropped by $100 at all GameStops"). Those writers should exercise careful news judgment to maintain the balance between informing readers about something that is truly newsworthy and falling for a company's PR gimmick. When in doubt, consult an editor.
>
> As columnists and beat writers reflect on merchandise, restaurants or services, they should avoid issuing a "call to action"—a suggestion that a reader purchase something or use only a specific store. For example, a blogger who reviews a new children's stroller or a fast hard drive might discuss quality and

cost of the merchandise, but stop short of suggesting that a particular store has the best prices or that readers should act specifically at their urging to make a type of purchase. Links to review articles on Twitter, Facebook, or other social media sites should be neutral, so that consumers benefit from the full context of the review, rather than a snapshot that can be misconstrued as an advertisement. They should also include language that makes it clear the article is a review. When in doubt, consult an editor.

But in the digital world, where thousands of "citizen journalists," "Mommy Bloggers," and amateur restaurant critics abound, the operating principles are much less clear. As Perlmutter and Schoen have observed, bloggers may plagiarize or fabricate material, misrepresent their identities or affiliations, or accept money or other consideration from commercial interests or advocacy groups without disclosing it, creating the impression that they are "independent local voices." Although a "blogger" code of ethics might, in theory, help to address these issues, they point out that many bloggers consider ethics codes to be a vestige of "old media" and antithetical to their missions, quoting Markos Moulitsas Zuniga, author of the Daily Kos blog, as saying ". . . if I was a journalist, I'd be breaking half the canon of journalistic ethics. . . . I am the epitome of conflict of interest, but at least I don't pretend otherwise" (Perlmutter & Schoen, 2007, p. 44).

If this were purely a matter of journalism ethics, these bloggers could, presumably, carry on as they wish without any legal ramifications, leaving it to their readers and viewers to assess their credibility and independence for themselves. But in December 2009, after an extended period for public comment, the Federal Trade Commission promulgated guidelines governing endorsements and testimonials in advertising. The impetus for the commission's action was a growing concern about "sponsored blogging"—bloggers or social media users who write about products or services in exchange for some form of compensation without disclosing that they have received it, potentially misleading viewers who assume that the review was an independent one. In the view of the Commission, these postings are presumed to be "sponsored advertising messages," which must be subject to regulation in order to protect unwary consumers. As fashion blogger Yuli Ziv told the Associated Press, "It's been an issue, regardless of the FTC. It's about trust" (Yao, 2009).

## THE FTC'S GUIDELINES ON SPONSORED BLOGGING

The FTC's guidelines establish specific transparency requirements, including affirmative disclosures that must accompany reviews, endorsements and testimonials identifying any "material connection," including cash or other in-kind payments, that exists between the blogger and the company that produces or sells the product or service in question. In addition, the digital reviewer will be liable for any false, misleading, or unsubstantiated claim about a product or service. These requirements apply not only to the blogger or other writer, but to any endorser, as well as to the advertiser, producer or seller. Indeed, the onus to monitor bloggers' disclosure actually rests with the company itself, and all can face enforcement penalties, including fines, for failure to comply.

Although technically the "Guides" are not binding law in themselves, they can be used by the FTC in pursuing enforcement actions—and have been.

The first such investigation involved Ann Taylor LOFT and "compensated bloggers" who had attended a preview fashion show and who were encouraged to blog about the show in order to win a $10 gift card. Some of those bloggers failed to disclose the incentive, and the FTC launched its investigation. Although it elected not to engage in any formal enforcement action, the Commission nevertheless emphasized, in an April 2010 letter to the lawyer for Ann Taylor Stores, that "material connections" must be disclosed, sending the message that it would pursue such cases in the future (Ann Taylor, 2010).

A second investigation did result in an enforcement proceeding against public relations agency Reverb Communications. The agency had been hired by video game application developers, and between November 2008 and May 2009, its employees posted reviews about the games on Apple's iTunes store, giving the impression that the reviews had been written by customers, not disclosing that they were hired to promote the game and even received a percentage of sales. The FTC concluded that Reverb was liable for failing to disclose this "material connection." To avoid the imposition of civil penalties, the parties agreed to a settlement in August 2010. Under its terms, Reverb was required to remove endorsements that might be misleading, and was prohibited from making further user claims unless they disclosed the connections in full. In the press release announcing entry of the consent order, Mary Engle, the director of the Commission's Division of Advertising Practices, stated that "Companies, including public relations firms involved in online marketing, need to abide by long-held principles of truth in advertising. Advertisers should not pass themselves off as ordinary consumers touting a product, and endorsers should make it clear when they have financial connections to sellers" (Reverb, 2010).

## MONITORING SPONSORED BLOGS

A third enforcement action in 2011 also resulted in a consent order, but with far more significant consequences for the company involved. Legacy Learning Systems, Inc., a company that produced the "Learn and Master Guitar Program," had solicited online endorsements by affiliates of "Review Ad," who advertised the program through blog posts, articles, and other materials linking to Legacy's web site, and received commissions for sales of Legacy's instructional materials. The affiliates posed as ordinary consumers and some failed to disclose their relationship with the company, even though Legacy required its affiliates to sign a contract promising to comply with the FTC guidelines. The Commission concluded that Legacy's failure to implement a monitoring program to ensure that they did so was a violation of the guidelines in itself. Specifically, it found that the reviews were false and misleading, and that Legacy's failure to correct the practices constituted "unfair and deceptive practices" in violation of Section 5(a) of the Federal Trade Commission Act.

In June 2011, the company was assessed a civil penalty of $250,000, and agreed to establish a monitoring program requiring it to rigorously monitor its affiliates' activities to ensure compliance, terminating and stopping payments to any affiliates who failed to make the requisite clear and prominent disclosure. The extensive and burdensome requirements coupled with the penalty clearly signaled that the FTC was serious about enforcing the guidelines (Legacy Learning, 2011).

Later that same year, in anticipation of the 2012 Super Bowl, the FTC issued an opinion in November 2011 regarding advertising practices leading up to the previous championship football game. Its investigation concerned auto manufacturer Hyundai, which had offered gift certificates to bloggers in exchange for posting links to forthcoming Super Bowl video advertisements or for commenting on the advertisements. Although only a small number of bloggers received the gift certificates, and some of those actually did disclose that they had, the focus of the Commission's investigation was whether or not Hyundai had actually instructed the bloggers to disclose their compensation to their viewers.

Although the FTC found that the guidelines had been violated, it declined to penalize Hyundai, noting that the campaign was actually executed by employees of a hired outside media firm that had failed to fully disclose the details of the program to the automaker. In fact, Hyundai already had a written compliance policy in place, binding on its agents, specifically prohibiting conduct of this kind, and the media company itself took prompt action to address the violations once it learned of them. Commentators noted that regulatory agencies "place considerable weight on whether a company had a compliance program in place when deciding whether to impose civil fines" or criminal penalties (Maxman & Magovern, 2012).

## SPONSORED BLOGGING DISCLOSURE REQUIREMENTS

It is significant that the government takes into account these types of self-regulatory schemes, which can serve to mitigate, or aggravate, the penalties that might be imposed. This is especially so because of the FTC's perception that the "traditional media" have such systems in place, whereas the typical "consumer-generated media" outlet does not.

This distinction was set forth in the FTC's Overview of the Commission's Review of the Guidelines, published along with the final rule in the Federal Register in October 2009:

> The Commission acknowledges that bloggers may be subject to different disclosure requirements than reviews in the traditional media. In general, under usual circumstances, the Commission does not consider reviews published in the traditional media (*i.e.*, where a newspaper, magazine or television or radio station with independent editorial responsibility assigns an employee to review various products or services as part of his or her official duties, and then publishes those reviews) to be sponsored advertising messages. Accordingly, such reviews are not "endorsements" within the meaning of the Guides. Under these circumstances, the Commission believes, knowing whether the media entity that published the review paid for the item in question would not affect the weight consumers give to the reviewer's statements. Of course, this view could be different if the reviewer were receiving a benefit directly from the manufacturer (or its agent).
>
> In contrast, if a blogger's statement on his personal blog or elsewhere (*e.g.* the site of an online retailer of electronic products) qualifies as an "endorsement—*i.e.*, as a sponsored message—due to the blogger's relationship with the advertiser or the value of the merchandise he has received and has been asked to review by the advertiser, knowing these facts might affect the weight consumers give to his review.

Predictably, this distinction unleashed a wave of protest from bloggers, who claimed they were being unfairly singled out to make affirmative disclosures not required of traditional media (Vilaga, 2009). Representative of this backlash was an "open letter" sent to FTC chairman Jon Leibowitz by Randall Rothenberg, President and CEO of the Interactive Advertising Bureau, a few days after the final guidelines were published.

Rothenberg conceded that false and deceptive advertising can and should be regulated. But he argued that although bloggers and other users of social media—which he calls "conversational media"— do not expect to be treated differently from "incumbent media," they "should be accorded the same rights and freedoms of other communications channels." Predicting that the Commission's rules would "specifically shackle online media while exempting our offline cousins and competitors from equivalent constraint," Rothenberg contended that by drawing this distinction between different forms of media, the rules would violate the First Amendment to the U.S. Constitution (Rothenberg, 2009).

## DEGREES OF SPONSORSHIP DIVIDE BLOGGERS AND LEGACY MEDIA REVIEWERS

In an interview with blogger Edward Champion, one of the FTC's assistant directors, Richard Cleland, attempted to clarify the Commission's rationale. The distinction, Cleland said, rested in the "degree of relationship between the advertiser and the blogger," and specifically, whether that relationship includes what the FTC would consider to be "compensation." In the Commission's view, a blogger who receives a free review copy of a book from a publisher has been "compensated," which would create an incentive to write a favorable review regardless of what she actually thought of the book. That blogger would be required to disclose that on her site if she keeps the book, posts an advertisement for it, or provides a link to Amazon's web site. "We are distinguishing who receives the compensation and who does the review. In the case where the newspaper receives the book and allows the reviewer to review it, it's still the property of the newspaper. Most newspapers have very strict rules about that and on what happens to those products." Cleland said (Champion, 2009).

Critics contend that the FTC is missing the point, especially if its true goal is to protect the consumer from being deceived about the independence of the reviewer. For example, Goldstein suggests that "[t]he question one should be asking is not what happens to the book after it is reviewed. Rather, the FTC should be asking itself: does a consumer expect that a blogger actually purchased a book or does it realize that a blogger received the book from the publisher, just like a newspaper reviewer?" (Goldstein, 2011).

Other commentators go further. The author of an unsigned review of the Guides in the Harvard Law Review argued that the compelled publication of a disclosure statement would have an "inherently pejorative connotation" which would undermine the writer's message. Moreover, holding bloggers to a higher standard than the legacy media based on a perception that the latter exercise "independent editorial responsibility" is legally unprecedented as well as fundamentally flawed because the receipt of paid advertising might actually create a greater conflict of interest than receipt of a book. Allowing the government to discriminate between different media based on such perceptions would allow the government to "manipulate the 'marketplace of ideas' just as direct interference with editorial content would." The author, therefore, echoes Rothenberg's assertions that the Guides are unconstitutional (Recent Regulation, 2010, p. 123).

## DIFFERING REGULATION BASED ON MEDIA TYPE

However, this analysis overlooks or minimizes the reality that the Supreme Court of the United States has upheld different forms of government regulation based on the type of media involved. For example, the author concedes that more comprehensive regulation of the broadcast media has been upheld based on "scarcity" of frequencies in the broadcast spectrum, but fails to mention that another justification for such regulation is based on the federal Communications Act's requirement that broadcast licensees operate to advance the "public interest, convenience or necessity" (Communications Act of 1934). Similar rationales arguably apply to government attempts to prevent and punish speech that is deemed to be deceptive advertising.

Nevertheless, it is also true that the Supreme Court has ruled that speech on the Internet is entitled to the same First Amendment protection that would apply to the print media (Reno v. ACLU, 1997). In that context, is there any justification for the FTC to draw the distinction it does? Should the government undertake to set ethical standards for the media?

The answer, at least from a legal perspective, is mixed. When asked to determine the constitutionality of a Florida statute that required newspapers to grant a right of reply to political candidates who were attacked "in its columns" or face criminal penalties, the Supreme Court struck it down. The opinion by Chief Justice Warren Burger mused that compelled publication of content a newspaper would not otherwise choose to print violated its editorial independence. "A responsible press is an undoubtedly desirable goal, but press responsibility is not mandated by the Constitution and like many other virtues it cannot be legislated" (Miami Herald v. Tornillo, 1974). Similarly, in a libel suit based on a journalist's alleged alteration of a source's statements that she had placed in quotation marks, the Court ruled that, even though journalism ethics standards might be more stringent, editorial deviation from the exact words spoken would not be the equivalent of "actual malice" (knowledge of falsity or reckless disregard of the truth) as a matter of law unless the meaning of the actual statement has been materially changed—in other words, that the alteration changed the substance of what the speaker intended to convey (Masson v. *New Yorker Magazine*, 1991).

On the other hand, the Court did engage in what amounted to an ethical prescription in another case involving the decision of editors at two Twin Cities-based newspapers to overrule a reporter's oral promise of confidentiality to a source and to publish his name. The newspapers contended that the identity of the source—a political operative who provided information about minor criminal offenses about an opposing candidate for lieutenant governor—was the most important element of the story. After the articles appeared, the operative was fired from his job with the gubernatorial campaign, and sued under the theory of promissory estoppel, a generally-applicable law which permits individuals who have been harmed when a promise on which they relied is broken to file a civil lawsuit seeking monetary damages. The newspapers contended that applying the law to them amounted to holding them legally liable for an editorial decision to publish truthful information, and would violate their First Amendment rights. But as Justice Byron White put it, the parties had voluntarily entered into the agreement restricting these rights, and "Minnesota law simply requires those making promises to keep them." And indeed, traditional news media ethical guidelines almost invariably require journalists to do just that. For example, the Society of Professional Journalists' (SPJ) Code of Ethics urges journalists to be cautious before promising a source anonymity and to "[c]larify conditions attached to any promise made in exchange for information," but ultimately, to "[k]eep promises" (SPJ Code, 1996).

Many online news media practitioners cite the SPJ Ethics Code, but others have attempted to draft their own. In 2006, for example, the Poynter Institute convened a conference to create a set of ethical guidelines. Perhaps not surprisingly, many of the principles were similar to those listed in the SPJ Code. For example, the SPJ Code, under the heading "Act Independently," exhorts journalists to "Avoid conflicts of interest, real or perceived," to "Refuse gifts, favors, fees, free travel and special treatment," and to "Disclose unavoidable conflict." The Poynter Guidelines similar urge "Journalists [to] honor the principle of independence. They should avoid conflicts of interest or the appearance of conflicts that could imperil their ability to report or the credibility of their reporting or commentary. They should not accept gifts or favors from people or entities they cover or over whom they might influence coverage" (Online Journalism Ethics, 2007).

But as the Supreme Court has observed, turning voluntary and aspirational media ethics precepts into legally-binding and enforceable obligations is rarely justified, as well as constitutionally questionable in light of the American tradition that prohibits Congress or any other legislative body to enact laws that abridge press freedom. But assuming that the FTC Guides could withstand constitutional scrutiny, are there steps bloggers could or should take to minimize their legal risk?

## BLOGGING WITH INTEGRITY

One available option is offered by the "Blog with Integrity" web site. Blog with Integrity was created by four bloggers in July 2009, "[a]fter a spring and early summer of polarizing debates about blogger compensation, sponsored posts and product reviews, an alarming increase in ethical lapses and idea theft, and a growing backlash against poor blogger relations practices" (Blog with Integrity, 2009). A "Blog with Integrity" pledge is posted online, and social media users may sign the pledge and/or display a "Blog with Integrity" badge on their own web sites. In relevant part, those who sign the pledge promise to "disclose material relationships, policies and business practices. My readers will know the difference between editorial, advertorial, and advertising, should I choose to have it. If I do sponsored or paid posts, they are clearly marked" (Blog with Integrity, 2009).

The Blog with Integrity site has inspired imitators. In July 2009, "Trisha," administrator of the MomDot.com web site, observed that "Mom Bloggers have turned from what they love the most, their family, into working directly as public relations for their captive audience. . . . While we adore many of our fabulous PR reps . . . we are inundated with hundreds, if not thousands, of product requests each year resulting in massive obligations and deadline stress." She called for a PR Blackout for the week of August 10-16 "where you do not blog ANY giveaways, ANY reviews, and Zero press releases" (P.R. Blackout Challenge, 2009). The motivation seemed to be to refocus the "Mommy Bloggers" on their core mission of blogging about "basics," rather than by ethical concerns.

Nevertheless, the founder of the "British Mummy Bloggers" social network in the United Kingdom and author of the "A Modern Mother" blog, noting that the FTC was on the cusp of issuing its guidelines, exhorted her peers to "make sure the same thing doesn't happen here." She opined that "British mummy bloggers don't need a code of ethics," which, she wrote, "would take all the fun out of blogging and make it seem more like work." But she did suggest that "we could all use a reminder of the issues of ethical blogging," and created a "British Mummy Bloggers Do It With Integrity" badge. The principles those who post the badge agree to include "Make transparent any relationships with products or companies," "Clearly label advertising, advertorials and/or sponsored posts," and "Always write as truthfully as possible about a product or a company." As with the original Blog with Integrity pledge and badge, participation is voluntary. And significantly, as "A Modern Mother" notes, "we cannot guarantee compliance" (British Mummy Bloggers, 2009).

For traditional journalists who have long tried to follow media ethics standards, regardless of the platform in which they work, these cavalier dismissals of articulated principles may seem jarring. And it could be argued that it is precisely this lack of appreciation of the need for honesty, disclosure and transparency that motivated the FTC to start policing consumer-generated media in the first place.

For the moment, the FTC seems determined to continue its enforcement actions. Undoubtedly it will do so selectively, since it is impossible for the Commission to oversee all of the thousands of bloggers and millions of Tweeters who post product and services reviews on the Internet. Based on its actions to date, it appears that the Commission will concentrate most of its enforcement efforts on the companies or agencies that supply the incentives to bloggers.

But the Commission reserves the right to pursue bloggers as well, although the FTC's Cleland has stated that the focus would be on "repeat offenders" who continue to post reviews without disclosing material connections after warnings to stop. As attorney Richard Newman wrote, "Make no mistake about it—the Final Guidelines are not for show. . . . A blogger is also liable if he/she fails to disclose clearly and conspicuously that he/she is being paid for his/her services. In order to limit potential liability, all those in the marketing stream should ensure that bloggers are provided with guidance and training concerning the need to ensure that statements they make are truthful and substantiated. Advertisers and networks should also monitor bloggers who are being paid to promote its products and take steps necessary to halt the continued publication of deceptive representations when they are discovered" (Newman, 2012).

All of which suggests that the most important principle that bloggers and their sponsors can embrace to avoid FTC sanctions is also one of the most fundamental: transparency. This may be one of those rare situations where the law and ethics act in harmony to promote the free flow of information and the exchange of ideas.

## REFERENCES

Alexander, L. (2009, June 11). AP reporter busted for saying on Facebook that sun rises in East. *Blog on the run: Reloaded.* Retrieved from https://blogontherun.wordpress.com/2009/06/11/ap-reporter-busted-for-saying-on-facebook-that-sun-rises-in-east/

Associated Press. (2012, January). Social media guidelines for AP employees. Retrieved from http://www.ap.org/Images/SocialMediaGuidelinesforAPEmployees-RevisedJanuary2012_tcm28-4699.pdf

Austin American-Statesman (n.d.). Ethics code for *Austin American-Statesman*—news/editorial employees. Retrieved from http://www.statesman.com/news/ethics-code-for-austin-american-statesman-news-editorial-284590.html

Blog with Integrity. (2009). Retrieved from http://www.blogwithintegrity.com/

British mummy bloggers do it with integrity (2009, Aug. 14). *A Modern Mother.* Retrieved from http://www.amodernmother.com/2009/08/british-mummy-bloggers-do-it-with-integrity.html

Champion, E. (2009, Oct. 5). Interview with the FTC's Richard Cleland, Edrants. Retrieved from http://www.edrants.com/interview-with-the-ftcs-richard-cleland

*Cohen v. Cowles Media Co.*, 501 U.S. 663 (1991).

*Communications Act of 1934*, 48 Stat. 1064 (1934), as amended, 47 U.S.C.A. § 151 et seq. (April 1, 1996).

Dugan, M. (2008). Journalism ethics and the Independent Journalist, *McGeorge Law Review* (39), 801-811.

Empson, R. (2011, May 23). Jeff Jarvis: when it comes to new journalism, "Transparency is the new objectivity". *TechCrunch*. Retrieved from http://techcrunch.com/2011/05/23/jeff-jarvis-when-it-comes-to-new-journalism-transparency-is-the-new-objectivity/

Engle, M. (2010, April 20). Letter to Kenneth A. Plevan, counsel for Ann Taylor Stores Corp. Retrieved from http://www.ftc.gov/os/closings/100420anntaylorclosingletter.pdf

Federal Trade Commission. (2009). Guides concerning the use of endorsements and testimonials in advertising. *Federal Register*, 74 (198), 53124-53143. Retrieved from http:// www.ftc.gov/os/2009/10/091005revisedendorsementguides.pdf

Federal Trade Commission. (2010, Aug. 26). Public relations firm to settle FTC charges that it advertised clients' gaming through misleading online endorsements. Retrieved from http:// www.ftc.gov/opa/2010/08/reverb.shtm

Gahran, A. (2009, May 15). News organizations implement new social media guidelines. *E-Media Tidbits*. Retrieved from http://www.poynter.org/how-tos/digital-strategies/e-media-tidbits/95792/news-organizations-implement-new-social-media-ethics-policies/

Getgood, S. (2010, April 2). Eleven urban myths about the FTC guidelines for endorsements & testimonials. *Blog Her*. Retrieved from http://www.blogher.com/eleven-urban-myths-about-ftc-guidelines-endorsements-testimonials

Goldstein, J. (2011). How new FTC guidelines on endorsement and testimonials will affect traditional and new media. *Cardozo Arts & Entertainment Law Journal*, 28 (609), 609-629.

Hohmann, J. (2011, May), 10 best practices for social media: Helpful guidelines for news organizations. Retrieved from http://asne.org/portals/0/publications/public/10_best_practices_for_social_media.pdf

*In the Matter of Ann Taylor Stores Corp.*, (2010) FTC File No. 102-3147.

*In the Matter of Legacy Learning Systems*, (2011), FTC Dkt. No. C-4323 (settlement order). Retrieved from http://www.ftc.gov/os/caselist/1023055/110610legacylearningdo.pdf

*In the Matter of Reverb Communications, Inc.*, (2010), FTC Dkt. No. C-4310. Retrieved from http://www.ftc.gov/os/caselist/0923199/101126reverbdo.pdf

Kramer, S. (Sept. 27, 2009). WaPo's social media guidelines paint staff into virtual corner; Text full of guidelines. *Paid Content*. Retrieved from http://paidcontent.org/2009/09/27/419-wapos-social-media-guidelines-paint-staff-into-virtual-corner/

*Masson v. New Yorker Magazine, Inc.*, 501 U.S. 496 (1991).

Maxman, M. & Magovern, R. (2012, Jan 24). From the experts: Super Bowl ads meet corporate compliance. *Corporate Counsel*. Retrieved from http://www.law.com/jsp/cc/PubArticleFriendlyCC.jsp?id-1202539637394

May British mummy bloggers never need a PR blackout! (2009, July 15). *A Modern Mother*. Retrieved from http://www.amodernmother.com/2009/07/may-we-never-have-a-pr-blackout-in-the-uk.html

McCullagh, D. (2009, Oct. 8). FTC blogging rules draw online protests. Retrieved from http://www.cbsnews.com/blogs/2009/10/08/taking_liberties/entry5372890.shtml

*Miami Herald v. Tornillo*, 418 U.S. 241 (1974).

News Blogs and Online Columns. (2009) *New York Times*. Retrieved from http://asne.org/Article_View/ArticleId/312/The-New-York-Times-News-Blogs-and-Online-Columns.aspx

Newman, R. (2012, Jan. 20). How to guarantee the FTC will bust you. *Performance Marketing Insider*. Retrieved from http://performinsider.com/2012/01/how-to-guarantee-the-ftc-will-bust-you/

Online journalism ethics: Guidelines from the conference. (2007, Feb 11). Retrieved from http://www.poynteronline.org/content/content_print.asp?id=117350

Perlmutter, D. & Schoen, M. (2007). "If I break a rule, what do I do, fire myself?": Ethics codes of independent blogs. *Journal of Mass Media Ethics*, 22 (1), 37-48.

Podger, P. (2009, June/July). The limits of control. *American Journalism Review*. Retrieved from http://www.ajr.org/article_printable.asp?id=4798

Poniewozik, J. (2010, Nov. 29). The end of "objectivity." *Time*. Retrieved from http://www.time.com/time/printout/0,8816,2032138,00.html

PR blackout challenges mom bloggers to return to basics. (2009, July 14). *Marketing VOX*. Retrieved from http://www.marketingvox.com/pr-blackout-challenges-mom-bloggers-to-return-to-basics-044614/

Recent regulation: Internet law—advertising and consumer protection. (2010). *Harvard Law Review*, 123, 1540-1547.

*Reno v. American Civil Liberties Union*, 521 U.S. 844 (1997).

Roderick, K. (2010, June 22). L.A. *Times* punishes pressroom blogger. *LA Observed*.

Rothenberg, R. (2009, Oct. 15). Randall Rothenberg's open letter to FTC. Retrieved from http://www.iab.net/public_policy/openletter-ftc

Society of Professional Journalists. (1996). Code of Ethics. Retrieved from http://www.spj.org/pdf/ethicscode.pdf

Strupp, J. (2009, June 23). New AP social media policy draws union fire. *Editor & Publisher*. Retrieved from http://www.editorandpublisher.com/eandp/news/article_display.jsp?vnu_content_id=1003986853

Strupp, J. (2010a, April 8). Philly guild blasts social networking policy. *Media Matters for America*. Retrieved from http://mediamatters.org/print/strupp/201004080040

Strupp, J. (2010b, Oct. 14). *Star-Ledger* editor warns staffers about social media comments. *Media Matters for America*. Retrieved from http://mediamatters.org/print/strupp/201010140011

Sullivan, W. (2009, May 14). News organizations implement new social media ethics policies. Retrieved from http://www.poynter.org/how-tos/digital-strategies/e-media-tidbits/95792/news-organizations-implement-new-social-media-ethics-policies/

"Trisha," (2009, July 13). P.R. blackout challenge. *Mom Dot Com*. Retrieved from http://www.momdot.com/pr-blackout-challenge

*U.S. Constitution, Amendment I.*

Vilaga, J. (2009, Oct. 16). FTC sticks to its regulations as blogger backlash builds, *Fast Company*. Retrieved from http://www.fastcompany.com/blog/jennifer-vilaga/slipstream/backlash-grows-blogosphere

Weinberger, D & Schotz, A. (2010, Oct. 8). Is transparency the new objectivity? *CQ Researcher*. 20 (15), 837.

Yao, D. (2009, June 21). FTC plans to monitor blogs for claims, payments. *Associated Press*. Retrieved from http://abcnews.go.com/Technology/story?id=7899371&page=2

# Index

# About the Contributors

**Berrin Beasley** is associate professor of communication at the University of North Florida. Dr. Beasley works in the areas of media ethics, the media's portrayal of women, and journalism history. Her research has been published in numerous journals and books.

**Paul Bloomfield** is associate professor of philosophy at the University of Connecticut (Storrs). His areas of specialization are moral philosophy and metaphysics, and especially their overlap, a subdiscipline known as "meta-ethics." He is the author of *Moral Reality* (2001) and editor of *Morality and Self-Interest* (2008), as well as numerous articles concerning morality, virtue, metaphysics, and epistemology. He is currently working on a new book, tentatively titled "A Theory of the Good Life," in which he argues that immorality is inescapably harmful to those who engage in it and that, as humans, we will always be as happy as possible, given our circumstances, by being as virtuous as we can possibly be.

**Kathy Brittain Richardson** is professor of communication at Berry College, where she teaches courses in media law and ethics, public relations and communication theory. From 1999 until 2009 Richardson served as associate provost and dean of academic services, and in 2008–2009 as interim provost, at Berry College. She is a coauthor of *Media Ethics: Cases and Moral Reasoning*, now in its ninth edition, and the coauthor of *Applied Public Relations: Cases in Stakeholder Management*, now in its second edition. She serves as the editor of *Journalism & Communication Monographs*. Her research interests include media ethics, product placement, music videos, and student expression. She earned a master's degree in journalism and the Ph.D.

in mass communication from the Grady College of Journalism and Mass Communication at the University of Georgia and a bachelor's degree in communication and religion and philosophy from Shorter College.

**Deni Elliott** holds the Eleanor Poynter Jamison Chair in Media Ethics and Press Policy at the University of South Florida. Prior to moving to Florida in 2003, she taught ethics in Philosophy or Journalism departments or served as founding director for the ethics center (or all of the above) at Utah State University, Dartmouth College, and the University of Montana. Deni is the author or editor of seven books, more than one hundred scholarly articles and book chapters, and more than one hundred pieces for the trade press—all in some area of practical ethics, mostly in media.

**Mitchell R. Haney** is associate professor of philosophy and director of the BlueCross/BlueShield Center for Ethics, Public Policy and the Professions at the University of North Florida. He works in the areas of ethical theory, meta-ethics, and business ethics. Dr. Haney is the coeditor, with A. David Kline, of *The Value of Time and Leisure in a World of Work* (2010). He is also the author of articles such as "The Value of Slowness" (2010), "On the Need for Theory in Business Ethics" (2009), and "Changes in Latitude, Changes in Attitudes" with Peter French (2005). He is presently working on a book titled *Slowness and the Ethics of Living*.

**Jane Kirtley** is the Silha Professor of Media Ethics and Law at the School of Journalism and Mass Communication at the University of Minnesota, where she directs the Silha Center for the Study of Media Ethics and Law and is an affiliated faculty member of the University of Minnesota Law School. Prof. Kirtley was executive director of The Reporters Committee for Freedom of the Press in Arlington, Virginia from 1985 to 1999. She writes and speaks frequently on media law and ethics issues, both in the United States and abroad. Prof. Kirtley serves on the boards of *Communication Law & Policy*, the *Journal of Media Law & Ethics*, and the Sigma Delta Chi Foundation, and is a member of the National SPJ Ethics Committee. Her honors include the Edith Wortman First Amendment Matrix Foundation Award and the John Peter Zenger Award from the University of Arizona. She is a member of the New York, Virginia and District of Columbia bars.

**Vance Ricks** is associate professor of philosophy at Guilford College. His research areas include ethics, friendship, and ethics and technology (including social media); he is also an avid thinker about how to best communicate philosophy. He is a regular contributor to blogs such as the Public Philosophy Network and In Socrates' Wake.

**Lee Wilkins** is a Curator's Teaching Professor at the University of Missouri School of Journalism, where she has taught since 1990. Her research and teaching interests focus on media ethics, and within that, moral decision making and the influences on it and media coverage of disasters and risk. Her coedited book with Clifford Christians, *The Media Ethics Handbook*, was named best edited book of 2009 by the ethics division of the National Communication Association. She has written numerous book chapters and articles on ethics, the most recent including "The Ethics of Professional Corruption" (in *Ethics & Evil in the Public Sphere*), "The Wages of Synergy"(with Elizabeth Hendrickson in *Journalism Practice*), "Covering Disasters: An Ethical Approach to News Reporting" (in *A Philosophical Approach to Journalism Ethics*, edited by Christopher Meyers), and "Connecting Care and Duty: How Neuroscience and Feminist Ethics Can Contribute to Understanding Professional Moral Development" (in *Media Ethics Beyond Borders: A Global Perspective*, edited by Stephen J. A. Ward & Herman Wasserman). She is married to David Black, a retired public school teacher, and is owned by two dogs and a canary named Dobby.